HOW TO SURVIVE A JEWISH MOTHER

(A Guilt-Written Guide)

by

R. STEVEN ARNOLD

Introduction by

HENNY YOUNGMAN

Illustrated by

BOB NELSON

CCC PUBLICATIONS

Published by

CCC Publications
1111 Rancho Conejo Blvd. • Suites 411 & 412
Newbury Park, CA 91320

Manufactured in the United States Of America

Cover © 1996 CCC Publications

Interior illustrations © 1996 CCC Publications

Cover and interior art by Bob Nelson

Cover/Interior production by Oasis Graphics

ISBN: 1-57644-005-2

If your local U.S. bookstore is out of stock, copies of this book may be obtained by mailing check or money order for $6.95 per book (plus $2.50 to cover postage and handling) to: CCC Publications; 1111 Rancho Conejo Blvd., Suites 411 & 412, Newbury Park, CA 91320.

Pre-publication Edition – 6/96

DEDICATION

To my beloved parents,
Matilda and Arnold,
without whose
consummation of love
and affliction,
this author would
not have been possible.

TABLE OF CONTENTS

INTRODUCTION
By HENNY YOUNGMAN

When Steve Arnold asked me to write an introduction to How To Survive a Jewish Mother, I was thrilled. I happened to be on a roller coaster ride in Disneyland at the time. But, even if my feet were firmly planted on terra cotta, I would have been thrilled to introduce this long overdue book. He has been writing it for thirty years.

I also happen to be an expert on the book's subject matter. I have survived a Jewish mother and have the guilt marks to prove it.

If you don't believe me you can check the birth records at London Jewish Hospital for March 2, 1906. You'll see the name Henry Finkelstein. He was in the crib next to mine and will testify as to my whereabouts.

You may wonder how come I was born in London, England. Well, it was convenient. My mother was there at the time. I understand she had a difficult delivery. I was glad I was able to be with her when she was going through all that pain.

It wasn't an easy delivery for me either. We had a nearsighted doctor. When he held me up and slapped me, he almost broke my nose.

In those days deliveries were quite painful. They didn't have the incredible advancements in medical techniques we have today. A few years from now people will most likely conceive over the Internet, and the baby will be delivered the next morning by Fed Ex.

My mother brought me to America when I was six months old. At the time, I didn't speak a word of English. She also brought along my father. Someone had to go out and make a living.

They say Jewish mothers are protective of their children. Not mine. When I wanted to play sports in high school, momma was not afraid of my getting hurt. Actually, I did quite well at school sports . I was the second best high jumper on the girl's track team. I think the girl that was better than me was on steroids.

Growing up in Brooklyn, I was sent to Hebrew school like every other Jewish boy in the neighborhood. And when I became thirteen, I had my Bar Mitzvah. Bar Mitzvah is Yiddish for "give the little shmageggie a bunch of presents he can't use." I'm writing this introduction with the last of the fountain pens I received as a gift. I outgrew the blue serge suit last winter.

I remember standing in front of the pulpit at B'nai Israel Synagogue giving my Bar Mitzvah speech in Yiddish. I figured if I spoke very quickly, nobody would notice that I didn't understand a word I was saying. After the ceremony, I was congratulated by several of my parent's friends for the stirring speech. They thought I was reciting my mother's recipe for gefilte fish.

Momma was so proud of me. That's a wonderful

thing about Jewish mothers. No matter how much of a fool their child makes of himself, she thinks he's a star. So, I decided to become a comedian. With an audience like that, how could I miss.

The Bar Mitzvah experience taught me to deliver as many one liners as possible as quickly as possible. That way if a joke bombs, I'll be three jokes ahead before anyone realizes it wasn't funny. It just goes to prove the mouth is quicker than the ear. The same concept applies to Jewish mothers. I know several who are hard of hearing but not one who is hard of speaking.

The first thing you must do to survive a Jewish mother is to listen to her. For years as a youngster, I would get headaches in the morning. My mother kept telling me, "Henny, when you get out of bed, it's feet first."

But I don't want to give away all the secrets in How To Survive a Jewish Mother. Read on and learn for yourself.

CHAPTER 1

WOMB WITH A VIEW

B irth is a great equalizer. Hindu or Jew, black or white, rich or poor, we all share the same first breath experience of having our entire body pushed through an opening about the size of an eye of a needle. This is nature's way of telling us it's a tough life out there.

We are crudely evicted from the comfortable surrounding we have been luxuriating in for the past nine months. What ever happened to the three-day notice clause in our lease? Given the old heave-ho from our water bed, and on our birthday to boot.

First, the landlady turns off the water. Then we are pulled head first and naked into the cold world, a pair of forceps clamped around our ears. Forceps! Our introduction to man-made instruments. We have never seen them before and may never see them again unless we are serving spaghetti.

Some giant forces our five-inch skull through a two-inch opening. We come out looking like Humpty Dumpty — after he fell off the wall. Fortunately, we are half blind, so we can't tell we look the spitting image of a Star Trek Klingon's reflection in a fun house mirror.

Before we can even say "Oy vay!" we are held

upside down by some behemoth wearing a mask and rubber gloves to protect his identity. He gives us a good slap on the rump. An act of violence we later learn is copied by our parents, and occasionally prostitutes if we pay them fifty dollars extra.

Just when we think it's safe to go back in the water again, this Freddie Kruger character with the pale green mask and matching designer cap picks up a scalpel. This is the second man-made instrument we are introduced to. Without even a "pardon me," he proceeds to cut off this cord attached to our belly. How the hell are we going to call womb service now?

Our first thought is that we are going to be scarred for life. Then the real fear sets in. How are we going to survive? Who is going to feed us? Not a pleasant thought for someone who hasn't yet learned how to make dinner reservations.

Finally, the masked man sponges us off, wraps us in a cozy blanket, and places us in the arms of this really nice lady. We think ,"Well, it wasn't really that bad of an experience. After all, it's not the end of the world or anything." The truth is, for us, it's only the beginning.

CHAPTER 2

BIRTH RITES AND WRONGS

I should have realized what was in store for me when my mother tried to stop the obstetrician from cutting the umbilical cord. She argued it was a good way to keep me from getting lost. He cut it off anyway. So she asked for a doggie bag. She still keeps the cord in her drawer. Every now and then she gives it a twist, and I call home.

Sometimes I dream my mother sneaks into my room in the middle of the night, yanks off the covers and sticks the cord back on with Krazy Glue. Once, after I forgot to call to wish her a happy birthday, I dreamt the damned thing just burst from my stomach like a scene from "Alien." The nightmare got even worse. I dreamt Sigourney Weaver was my mother and I was a bottle baby. It was not a titillating thought.

Strange phenomenon, the umbilical cord. Physically gone, yet it remains like an invisible albatross around our midsection. It is as much a part of our body as our appendix, though of considerably less value. We can't see it, touch it, or smell it, yet it has a presence. It's very similar to the medical discovery called "phantom pain." The appendage is gone but the memory lingers on.

Everyone, regardless of their religious background, has an invisible umbilical cord still attached. It's just that Jewish cords are a lot shorter. And, we can't get rid of them any more than we can keep a Jehovah's Witness from ringing our doorbell at dinnertime.

But now, thanks to this book, you will better understand the invisible cords that bind you. As you read along, many of the childhood experiences set forth will be familiar to you. At last, you will be able to objectively examine how growing up with a Jewish mother has impacted your life. You may be surprised to find out you have a Jewish mother even though you aren't Jewish. For it is not the religion, but the mind set that makes a "Jewish mother."

By reading this book, you will develop an understanding of what makes a Jewish mother tick. And, with understanding comes forgiveness, acceptance, and the realization you are laying the same trip on your kids.

IT IS STRANGE how many of the incidents which have a major impact on our lives happen before we are born. I'm referring to those incidents which influenced our parents lives to the extent they changed the way they brought us up. All Jewish mothers have a closet full of these experiences. You will understand your life better if you find the key to this closet. Generally it's a skeleton key.

In my case, my mother lost a daughter in childbirth five years before I was born. This tragic incident has had a lasting effect on my life. My parents were so afraid something bad would happen to me they watched me every minute. They took my temperature twice a night. It was a real pain in the ass. If there was even a small cloud in the sky, I had to wear my rubbers. I didn't even know what sex was at the time.

And, this overprotectiveness does not end in childhood. To this day, my mother insists I keep training wheels on my Mercedes. I call this the "Watch out Legacy." Watch out or you'll catch a cold. Watch out or you'll get hurt. I've spent the better part of my life watching out for things that never happen because of a sister I never had. Talk about a double negative.

When you're raised by a Jewish mother, you don't realize that she is being overprotective. You think it's quite natural for her apron strings to be on a reel. My mother kept telling me not to take candy from strangers. For years I thought I was a covert diabetic. Until I got married, she insisted I sleep with the lights on. I thought she expected me to lay eggs. She put a drop of milk on her wrist to make sure it wasn't too hot for me to drink. And that was just last week.

CHAPTER 3

BORN WITH A SILVER IOU IN MY MOUTH

It was blistering cold that March 15, 1938 when I decided it was time to make an appearance. Three o'clock in the morning, a blizzard covering the city of New York, and I wanted to see it. Sure it was inconsiderate, but how was I supposed to know it would be so difficult to get a taxi in that weather.

For a time, I believed this self-indulgent behavior to be my first guilt-ridden act. However, after years of analysis, I realize how ridiculous that notion was. Now, I know my first guilt-ridden act happened a good nine months earlier.

I have no memory of the amorous night of my conception. I don't really know whether it was a romantic interlude at all. Yet, I prefer to think of myself as the product of a candle-lit dinner, rather than a quickie in the back seat of Dad's Pontiac. I am not criticizing people whose existence are the result of parking accidents. Some fine human beings have gotten their start that way. It is rumored Lee Iacocca and Henry Ford II were back seat babies.

Please don't misunderstand my point. I don't feel guilty because my Dad to-be made it with my Mom to-be. I didn't even know these folks at the time. We didn't become related until several minutes later. I just feel fortunate I didn't wind up on the seat cushion.

I often wonder what I was like as my father's sperm. How come I survived when all those around me bit the dust. Was I a better swimmer, or just lucky? Perhaps it had something to do with an unborn survival instinct. Or maybe just a good sense of direction. But, the fact remains, it must have been a disaster area in there. And, I was the sole survivor. What a burden to bear.

My mother was a real martyr during our pregnancy. She never misses an opportunity to tell me how much she suffered on my behalf. It is only right that I take responsibility, even though I didn't have an embryo of an idea of the pain I was causing her. Those months I spent in isolation were certainly a growing experience. Now I realize what a self-centered fetus I was. Always kicking about the living conditions. The truth is I owe my mother a debt of gratitude I can never fully repay for stomaching my mischievous behavior for three quarters of a year.

✡✡✡✡✡✡✡✡✡✡✡✡✡✡✡✡✡✡✡✡✡✡✡✡✡✡✡✡✡

SURVIVAL TIP #1

Surviving a Jewish Mother is a question of mind over matter. If you don't mind, it doesn't matter.

✡✡✡✡✡✡✡✡✡✡✡✡✡✡✡✡✡✡✡✡✡✡✡✡✡✡✡✡✡

CHAPTER 4

THE BRISS -
A TRUE SLICE OF LIFE

A Jewish male's first religious ritual, called B'rith Milah, is not one that he will quickly forget. Circumcision is a time-honored tradition benignly referred to as "the Briss." Since the baby is only eight days old during this "celebration," he really can't appreciate the delicious chopped liver being served. He is also too young to get the point of the ceremony. In actual fact, he loses it.

Today, for health reasons, circumcision is routinely performed on non Jews as well. But, they refer to it as a procedure rather than a celebration. The main difference being that Christian circumcisions are performed by actual physicians in hospitals. On the other hand, the Jewish celebration takes place in your home and is performed by a Mohel. A Mohel, pronounced "Moyl," is more often than not an elderly religious zealot sporting a long black beard, wearing thick eyeglasses and having no medical degree. He is not paid a fee for his services, and works strictly for gratuities.

The Mohel who circumcised me, three fingers Berkowitz, has moved his operations to Kenya where he is circumcising Jewish elephants. He finds the tips are bigger. Actually, he was forced to leave the States because the Lighthouse for the Blind canceled his malpractice insurance.

The question arises as to how these Mohels are trained? Is there a Mohel University? If so, my son would be an honor student. He is exceptional at cutting classes. And who is the public relations genius who came up with the term Mohel in the first place? He certainly made a mountain out of a Mohel.

I wouldn't want to get a manicure from someone called a Mohel, no less put the crown jewels in his hands. However, once you know that one of the Yiddish words for penis is "shmekel", mohel doesn't sound so bad. It's a cut above being called a Shmekologist.

It is interesting to note the Eskimo language has only one word for penis, and fourteen words for snow. The Yiddish language, on the other hand, has numerous words for penis, and only one for snow. This probably accounts for why you never hear an Eskimo calling anyone a putz.

There is a school of thought which maintains Mohels are really PLO operatives executing an ancient Arab plot. The story goes that at the time of the building of the Pyramids, eighteen and a half minutes of transcripts were mysteriously erased from the recorded conversations of the Egyptian Parliament. Two enterprising journalists from the Cairo Post, after meeting with a disgruntled ex-government official, code name Deep Canal, pieced together the following conversation:

Pharaoh: "That Red Sea shtick Moses did is really the last straw. A cheap theatrical stunt like that could make us the laughing stock of Babylonia. We have to come up with a way to get even. Anyone have a suggestion."

King Tut: "Yoh, Chief. I've got an idea. These Jews always resist authority. Just suppose we convince them that something really horrible is in their best interests. Then forbid them to do it. They'll do it just for spite.

Pharaoh: "Give me an example, Kid."

King Tut: "Well, uh, take that stale bread the commissary is stuck with. You know, that dry stuff that tastes like cardboard. We spread the rumor it saved thousands of Jews from starving after the Red Sea fiasco. Then, we forbid them to eat it, but of course they will. They'll choke on it, drink too much Manischewitz wine washing it down, and all die in chariot accidents on their way home."

Pharaoh: "Not bad, Kid. You're on the right track. But we can do better than that."

Queen Hatsepsut: "I've got it. What is the worst thing you guys can think of happening to you? Getting your John Henry cut off, right. Well, let's convince the Jews that it is their religious duty to do just that."

Pharaoh: "They are not that stupid. They wouldn't be able to procreate so who would they lay their guilt trips on. Even if we made it punishable by life imprisonment, they wouldn't do it. It just won't fly."

Queen Hatseput: "Well then, let's just convince them to cut off a small piece."

THROUGH THE AGES, circumcision has been met with violent suppression. The Selecicid Dynasty declared it punishable by death. The Romans established a special edict outlawing its practice. Yet, in spite of these threats to person and freedom, Jews have continued to maintain circumcision as one of their most sacred practices.

Today circumcision is performed as a preventative measure to avoid infection in the genital area. However, a Harvard University Medical School study found no lesser degree of infection in circumcised Jews than in those given a placebo by being hit hard on the schlong with a dull stick and told they had been circumcised.

Consequently, it is possible this tradition has another, perhaps subtler, purpose. After all, what is tradition but a way for the old to control the new. Jews use circumcision. Christians have their own wonderful tradition welcoming a new born to religion. Baptism. A celebration of life in which a Christian baby is either doused with or dunked in cold water before he has even passed his first life-saving test.

Perhaps both these wonderful traditions were first established to teach respect for one's elders. I should have figured it out when my mother picked me up immediately after my Briss and whispered in my ear, "That will teach you to listen to your mother and not cry all night long."

Contrary to popular belief, circumcision is not really a traumatic experience. For one thing, babies are nearsighted. They think the Mohel is merely cutting off a piece of the umbilical cord the masked man missed. Even if they knew it was a part of their penis, they would not be fazed. To a baby, it is simply an overflow valve with a directional nozzle. Since diapers present a large target, a shorter nozzle doesn't appear to be a drawback.

It is not until we become teenagers that we can appreciate this particular appendage has more than one function. And, in comparison to some of our gentile friends, we have come up a bit short. This revelation is particularly confusing to those of us who remember the Briss blessing, which begins with the words, "Blessed be he that cometh."

CHAPTER 5

CRIB NOTES

The average infant spends the first twenty months of its life in a crib. A few are let out a little early for good behavior. In truth, cribs are nothing more than baby jails. The inside of the average crib measures 27 inches by 51 inches. The distance between the crib slates must be no more than 2 3/8 inches apart in order to make sure the prisoner doesn't escape. We are sentenced to spend the early years of our life behind bars, and without even a trial. How discouraging. No sooner do we break out of solitary confinement than we are incarcerated again.

It is interesting to note in essentially all third world countries the infant sleeps in the mother's bed. However, Jewish mothers are particularly partial to cribs. In it, the baby is safe and sound. There is nowhere to go and nothing to do, except pee. My mother felt so secure when I was in my crib that she even took off my handcuffs.

Occasionally, when a baby has been good, it is taken out in a stroller. A stroller is another term for "jail on wheels." Lying on his or her back, there is no way a baby can see out of the stroller. Generally, it is looking straight up at the hood of the stroller. However, the purpose of a stroller is not for a baby to look out, but for people to look in. Once a Jewish mother elicits,

"What a cute baby" from six passersby, she can return home.

However, in spite of the claustrophobic atmosphere of cribs and strollers, it represents one of only two times in life we can lie on our back and have our relatives cater to our every whim. The other is on our deathbed. But only if we are extremely rich and in the process of changing our will.

The crib years are a vital time in our development. It affords us the opportunity to take in everything going on around us without having to respond. We become human sponges. Looking, listening, smelling, touching and passing wind indiscriminately. Nothing is expected of us except to look cute, which is easy since our hands and feet are so tiny.

We just lie there, sucking our pacifier, and thinking of the wonderful, stress-free life we are going to enjoy. I loved my all-day sucker. When it was in my mouth, I didn't have a care in the world. After a while, I guess my mother felt I was a malingerer. So, she took the pacifier away from me. I cried like a baby. My protest seemed to work because she gave it back. Little did I know she had dipped it in spot remover. It tasted worse than sour milk. Quickly, I spit the pacifier out and it landed on my dog, Spot. He disappeared. As did my pacifier sucking habit. From then on it would be thumbs up. At least I knew where they had been for the last hour.

As with all babies, I learned quickly that crying was a great communication tool. Whenever I was hungry, all I did was cry and a bottle full of warm milk instantly appeared. When I was lonely, I would cry and my mother would come and rock me to sleep. Boy, was I in control. It was as easy as taking candy from a grown-up. Truly, the crib period is one of the best times in our lives.

Then, one day we make the mistake of uttering a word. Usually, "Mama." Pretty soon we are expected to say "Dada." And, that is the end of our childhood. From now on things are expected of us. We no longer can lie around enjoying our surroundings in peace. We have to entertain the folks with long soliloquies like "Pee-pee, Mama."

Next, we are removed from our crib, and are expected to motor under our own power. It isn't easy for us to crawl. Our bodies are out of proportion and our coordination is non-existent. We pull our torso along like a sack of potatoes. Eventually, we learn it works better if we lift our abdomen off the floor. My mother taught me to crawl by pasting the picture of a bare breast on a stick which was tied to my forehead. I've been chasing after breasts ever since.

After a while, it's fun to crawl around on all fours. That is until we learn that furniture does not move out of the way for us. After a few head-on collisions, we realize our eyes have another purpose besides excreting tears. We can actually stop before bumping into objects and, sometimes, even move around them. The problem is every time we signal a turn, we fall on our face.

Just when we have mastered the art of crawling,

our mother wants us to walk. This nice lady who has cared for and nurtured us our entire life is turning into a Marine sergeant. Walk! Is she kidding! It's an accomplishment if we can lie on the floor without holding on. Walking requires a strange prerequisite. It's called standing. This is not an easy chore for someone who, until now, has spent an entire lifetime prone. Okay, we give it the old pre-nursery school try. This is not very difficult we think. Then, our mother lets go of our hands. We fall quicker than a hooker at a Shriner's convention.

Eventually, we start to move forward. But, nobody taught us how to stop. It's like going down an expert ski slope without knowing how to break. Wham! Again, right on our kisser. Let's go back to something we are really accomplished at. Crying. But, this woman is relentless. Placed back on our feet, we are put to the test again. Finally, as if by magic, we get the knack of it. Look mom, I'm upwardly mobile. Little do we realize we walk like a drunken penguin.

No sooner do we learn to walk than this same taskmaster wants us to pee where and when she tells us. Now this is surely contrary to natural law. Do you think a mother elephant tells her baby where to defecate. "No, not by that tree, Dumbo. Go over there in the bushes."

I don't mean to brag, but I was an ace at potty training. My mother cleverly began by first training my stuffed doll, Pluto, while I watched. It wasn't long before I got the hang of it; though it did take a while before I stopped lifting my leg on the piano.

Slowly, we begin to notice that mom is expecting an awful lot from us. She is telling us what to do and when and where to do it. She is taking over our life. We have lost our independence before we ever had it.

It is time to smarten up before we are totally controlled. We sharpen our senses and look for danger under every pamper. After a while, we can understand much of what our mother is talking about. Pretty soon the "What a good baby" turns into "Stop crying" and "Don't suck your thumb." Rules! This is becoming a nightmare.

At around this time we begin to develop reason. We figure out that if she thinks we don't understand what she is saying, she can't get us to do what she wants. So, at first we ignore her. Just smile and go about our business while she shouts. This works for a while, but finally, she gets desperate. Wham! A slap on the rump like we haven't felt since the day we were born. This silence isn't working. It's time for a new strategy.

It is at this point we decide it is time to speak up. But, in a language our mother can't comprehend. Maybe, if we fain communication, she will give up and let us live our life in peace. So we begin to talk in baby syllables. A "um me me a tu tu" here and a "de do va va" there.

It works. She loves it. And for a while, she forgets to dish out orders.

Obviously, she is not bi-lingual. We say "gime ga futo tada", which of course means "I'm cold", and she hands us the Teddy bear. You would think she would have the courtesy to learn baby talk before she had us. It's not like it takes an Einstein to speak baby talk. Any two-year old can do it. It's a universal language, for God sakes. Do you think a German baby says "nict da kimper, ya" and a Chinese baby says "ing go ga ho." Of course not. Every baby speaks the same language. In fact, our parents all spoke it when they were young. Now, for some strange reason, they can't remember a single word.

CHAPTER 6

YUPPIE, I'M UPWARDLY MOBILE

Walking is a child's first step towards independence. This mobility allows him to move from room to room within the house breaking whatever he wishes. Balance is still a bit tricky, and the falls are constant. But, it is a small price to pay for this new found autonomy.

Few of us can remember the day we first walked a few yards without falling down, but I'm sure it is an experience buried deep in the recesses of our minds. For one thing, the furniture no longer resembles the Empire State Building. Soon walking becomes a habit and we can't stop. Leave us alone for a moment and we're off and walking. It is truly wonderful walking with no predetermined destination in mind. We can't get lost that way.

As exciting as the freedom of movement was to me, it was equally distressing to my mother. It gave her something more to worry about. She wouldn't leave me alone for a second. She followed me around the house as if I was about to steal the silverware. I didn't even know what silverware was, no less where she hid it.

My mother devised different ways to keep me in her sight. First, she attached a bell around my neck.

Anytime I decided to pick up and move, the bell would warn her. One day I took the bell off, threw it down the toilet and hid in the closet. My mother almost drowned looking for me.

Next, she tied an elastic band around my waist. This gave me a real feeling of deja vu. The elastic band was eight feet long so I could roam to a point. However, if I ventured too far, too fast, I was slung back into her arms like a pin to a magnet. I learned an important lesson from that experience. When a Jewish mother gives you freedom, there is usually a string attached.

Talking is a child's second step towards independence. Not the babble designed to confuse our parents, but real language using adult words. It is like a water faucet with a worn washer. Once the words start to flow, nobody can turn them off. The words don't always follow in a way that makes a sentence, but that's a detail. Young children don't understand the rules of conversation anymore than the rules of the road. If they were behind the wheel of a car for the first time, they wouldn't pay attention to the traffic lights. It's the same with conversation. They don't have any idea that a period is supposed to end a sentence. In fact, they think a sentence is something they were pardoned from when they were let out of the crib.

It takes a while for a child to understand that conversation has two facets: talking and listening. Listening is much harder for a child to learn than talking, particularly if he doesn't like what he is hearing. Children develop the art of selective hearing. It will keep them in good stead once they get married.

In time, they learn to complete sentences. Oddly enough, their mother usually continues to prattle for another several months. This is particularly embarrassing at dinner parties when she asks the guests if they want some more "mush mush" and begins cutting their meat.

Once a child speaks in sentences, his learning curve rises dramatically. The Jewish mother usually takes this opportunity to expose her child to one of the most terrifying experiences imaginable. The Mishpocheh! Parents, grandparents, uncles, aunts, cousins all form part of the extended family Jews call "The Mishpocheh." I don't know about your Mishpocheh, but mine were nothing to write home about.

Uncle Lenny was one of my favorites. He would throw me up in the air and catch me in his arms. I would giggle with pleasure, unaware of the risk I was taking. He would always breathe some awful smelling stuff in my face. It wasn't until years later that I developed a taste for Johnny Walker.

Grandma Horowitz was another of my favorites. She was one of the few adults I ever met who knew how to speak baby talk. Unfortunately, she still spoke with a Russian accent so I missed a lot of what she was saying. Yet, she regaled me with tales of her life in "the old country." Once she told me of her father who was a fisherman on the Volga River in White Russia. He would leave home for months at a time to catch fish during the sturgeon season. The sturgeons could easily reach ten feet in length and weigh several hundred pounds. One day my great-grandfather hooked onto one of the largest sturgeons ever seen in those parts. It was a momentous struggle and just as old man Horowitz was pulling the huge fish into the boat, the sturgeon, with a powerful jerk, pulled my great grandfather out of the boat. He was never seen or heard from again.

For years afterwards, my grandmother searched in vain for her father, particularly in Beluga caviar cans.

I didn't care for Aunt Beckie that much. She smelled like a musty house and was as big as one, too. Whenever I heard Aunt Beckie's shrill voice at the front door, I would hide. There were not many good hiding places in our four-room apartment. Once she became aware of the usual places like under the bed or in the closet, I had to become more ingenious. My best hiding place was in my Dad's old raccoon coat, which hung in the hall closet. Because it was so big and bulky, I was able to climb in it while it was still on the hanger, and literally disappear from sight. It was a wonderful hiding spot, but getting out wasn't that easy. Once I got stuck in it until football season. Eventually my aunt would find me and smother me with kisses. I felt like throwing up, and usually followed my instincts. After a while, I found that peeing was equally effective and less tiring.

Speaking of peeing, this is a good time to discuss

bed-wetting. Dr. Ima Kibitz, the renowned Israeli pediatrician, states that all children wet their beds. Too much water before bedtime, a cold night, a case of nerves or just plain laziness can be the cause. By age three a child should have graduated from toilet training and be well on his way to bladder control. However, bed wetting can continue until a child reaches the age of six. If it persists past that point, she suggests a mother should consider seeking a doctor's advice.

In my particular case, I continued to wet my bed until I was eight. My mother was concerned and told me she was taking me to a child psychiatrist. I wondered what good that would do. The kid probably wets his bed, too.

The psychiatrist suggested several different cures for bed-wetting which my mother had to choose from. Unfortunately for me, she chose electric shock therapy. A rubber sheet, with narrow electric cords running through it, was placed under my cotton sheet. Every time I wet the bed, a small electric current would be emitted. At first, it was a rude awakening, but it did work. And, thank goodness, it did. After seeing James Cagney in "Public Enemy," I understood what would happen if I continued the bed wetting into adulthood.

SURVIVAL TIP #2

Create a standard answer to the question "Why don't you ever listen to your mother?" Make sure it is lengthy and involved. After she hears the same explanation time and again, she will get bored and stop asking.

Eg: Mother: "I told you you would get a stomach ache eating all that fruit. Why don't you ever listen to your mother?"

Daughter: "I think it is because of what happened when I was 5 years old. You remember the time Aunt Beckie came over for the weekend. She brought her toy poodle, what was its name, Fife, I think. Well, Fife kept trying to hump Uncle Irving's leg. Uncle Irving got so annoyed that he jumped up from his chair and knocked over your pretty blue vase. You asked me to clean it up and I cut my finger. Just about then Dad walked in with Mr. Wimple who tripped on..."

Mother: "Alright! Enough already."

CHAPTER 7

DON'T FENCE ME IN

Once a child can stand on his own two feet, it is time for him to explore the world outside. This is a terrifying period for the Jewish mother. Her child is an innocent in a world of deception and decadence. However, unless she wishes to bring up a recluse, she must expose him to real life sooner or later.

My mother chose later. Until I was four, she did not allow me to play with other children for fear I would catch something. So, being an only child, I had nobody to play with. We would go to the park and stay at the far end of the playground. All the other children were at the other end playing on the slides, swings and jungle jack. I guessed they weren't Jewish. All I had on my end of the playground was a see-saw. I would jump on one end and the see-saw would pitch my way. Quickly, I would dismount and run to the other side and get on. Then back to the other side and so on. Talk about circuit training.

After a while, my father bought me a boomerang so I could at least have a game of catch. It was defective. The first time I threw it, the boomerang just sailed to the other end of the playground. It was picked up and eaten by a dingo dog. My father was so angry that he sued the manufacturer. We lost. Dad said it was a kangaroo court.

Since I had no real friends, I made one up. I named him "Mo." In my mind, Mo was my height, weight and complexion. What distinguished him from me was his long, drooping ears, much like a basset hound. He also had a round, black, moist nose, which meant he was healthy. Mo only spoke with his eyes, and he was my best friend. As I met more friends my own age, I guess Mo got jealous, because one day he just left my life entirely. Ironically, he still sends me birthday cards.

Psychiatrists will tell you that all children have a natural tendency to create a fantasy world. The more they are sheltered, the more they create and maintain an imaginary life. The fantasy creation may take many forms, but the most typical is an imaginary friend with a name and full physical description. Most children will "lose" their imaginary buddy as they become more involved with their peers. In some rare instances, this self-deception can last until adulthood. It is termed the "Jimmy Stewart Syndrome."

Eventually, my mother decided she could no longer keep me isolated. It was time for me to meet other people, particularly those my own size. She had just three words of advice. "Hold my hand." I was introduced to our neighbor's kids, Jay and Herbie, who were about my age. This was after she examined their medical records thoroughly. It was a unique experience playing with other midgets. We had a lot of fun together. Every afternoon we would meet in the park and play Cowboys and Indians. I know now it's not politically correct to play that game. However, that was before "Dances with Wolves." At that time, Indians spelled trouble. They would rather scalp Gabby Hayes than win the World Series.

Herbie always wanted to play the Indian, which was okay with Jay and me. Obviously, the kid had a death wish. Jay would play the bad guy. This is because his mother had bought him a black cowboy hat. I played the role of the good guy, which should normally guarantee survival. However, it never seemed to work out that way. After about an hour of running around yelping and going bang-bang, Herbie would be lying on the ground dead as a doornail. Jay would come up to me and say, "This town isn't big enough for both of us." We would stand opposite each other, about ten feet apart, with our cap pistols holstered and ready. You could split the air with a knife. Suddenly, one of us would yell "Draw" and we would both reach for our six shooters. Jay would always beat me to the draw. But, I would have been much faster if my mother wasn't holding onto my hand.

The game I really liked to play with my new found friends was Hide and Seek. Thanks to my Aunt Beckie, I had become a great hider. In fact, I was so good at hiding, I had to leave subtle hints just to keep the game interesting. A muffled cough, an obvious shoe print or a dropped glove usually led to my capture. The glove clue was a bit difficult since my mother had attached them to my jacket sleeves with safety pins. Sometimes if Herbie was nearing the "ready or not-here I come" stage, I had to dispose of the glove with my jacket attached. It surprised everyone, after my capture, when the glove no longer fit. It must have been an Isotoner.

It is well established that a Jewish mother's overprotective and possessive behavior is interpreted by the child as a sign of love. The child thinks other mothers, who give their children more freedom, just don't care as much about their safety. It isn't until the child develops a relationship with the opposite sex that he begins to question his mother's motives.

As a child, it never occurred to me there were any women in the world except my mother. Every now and then, I played with little girls, but I just thought they were soft boys. It wasn't until I met my first love, Ruthie Krawitz, that I realized there might be a difference.

This first telling encounter with the opposite sex occurred in kindergarten. Seated across the aisle from me was the prettiest girl I had ever seen. She had dark black hair, cute little dimples and a space between her braces-bearing front teeth that you could drive a Hummer through. I fell head over heels for Ruthie. For a while I tried to ignore her, but it didn't work. She had a magnetism I couldn't resist. One day I built up all the courage I could muster. I snuck up behind her and dunked her pigtail in the inkwell. Boy, it felt good to express my emotions for the opposite sex. She cried for a while. But it was a great icebreaker and we wound up being the best of friends. We would spend every day together, me dunking and her crying. It was the perfect relationship. Then, one day she moved out of town. I thought I would never see her again.

But life is full of surprises. Just last year, when I was vacationing in Hawaii, I noticed a familiar figure walking along the beach. I probably wouldn't have recognized Ruthie at all if it weren't for her ink stained hair. And, she was still wearing braces. I thought this a bit strange since she now had false teeth. I snuck up behind her and dunked her hair in the ocean. She began to cry as always. It was a wonderful reunion until her husband ran over and beat the living daylights out of me.

When I was six, I first learned how to play "Doctor." I never really enjoyed the game. I think it was because my mother harbored such a distrust for the medical profession. So, while my chums were examining their female playmates' private parts for the Black Plague, I sat alone in my room figuring out how to sue them for malpractice. Truth is, I was just too shy. Every time Ruthie suggested we play Doctor, I would tell her to take two aspirin and call me in the morning. Then, I'd send her a bill.

The game which embarrassed me the most, however, was Spin the Bottle. I would pray the bottle would never end its spin pointing at me. When it did, I would immediately fake a diabetic fit. I finally had to give up the ploy when I developed an immunity to insulin.

CHAPTER 8

A THOROUGHFARE TO REMEMBER

The word "hovering" is not of Yiddish derivation, yet it has only two applications. Helicopters and Jewish mothers. The difference between the two is that helicopters eventually run out of gas. Jewish mothers are famous for hovering over their children. Their deep expression of love is communicated by worrying and nervousness.

The overinvolvement of Jewish mothers in their children's lives has several roots. For one, Jewish ideology, particularly in the 1940s and 50s, dictated that the father alone should support the family. My father did his job well. Perhaps too well. He almost got kicked out of the synagogue when the rabbi found out how much bacon he was bringing home.

A woman's maternal duty, at that time, was to stay home and raise the children. Yet, many were educated, intelligent women who chose to give up their own aspirations and professional ambitions for "the good of the family." In their children, particular their sons, they saw a means of displacing all their aspirations. If they didn't have the opportunity to become a doctor, then their son certainly would have, whether he could stand the sight of blood or not.

Second, the Jewish history of persecution and oppression has left a residual fear which causes a subliminal need to protect their offspring from the dangers of the outside world. This invisible anxiety dictates many a Jewish mother's excesses.

My mother's first overt signs of overprotection appeared when I came of school age. Perhaps everything would have gone smoothly were it not for one minor problem. In order for me to go to school, it was necessary for me to cross the street. And not just any street. Amsterdam Avenue stood between me and P.S. 87 like a moat protecting an ancient castle. In my mother's mind, the waters were full of hungry alligators, each wearing a LaCoste sport shirt with a small Jew embossed on the pocket.

In truth, Amsterdam Avenue was an imposing thoroughfare. Unlike most New York City streets, it had three lanes of traffic flowing in two directions. Also, there were trolley cars, buses and commercial trucks constantly barrelling their way uptown and downtown. In the middle of the thoroughfare stood a pedestrian island, a safe haven, which seemed to say "If you can make it here, you're halfway home."

My mother found a safe way for us to cross Amsterdam Avenue. She would take hold of me in one hand and place the other, the one facing traffic, high in the air with all five fingers extended. Then, without looking at the traffic, she would proceed to cross the street. This "I dare you to hit a defenseless mother and child" salute worked quite well. Often a motorist would salute back, though most of the time using only one digit.

Amsterdam Avenue became my mother's excuse for accompanying me to school every morning. I tried to tell her I was old enough to go alone, but to no avail. What disturbed me most was, not my mother's overprotectiveness, but the razzing I received from my grade school classmates. "Mama's Boy" and "Little Stevie Weevie" were constant reminders of my plight. Finally, I persuaded my mother to let me proceed to school alone after we safely traversed Amsterdam Avenue. It was, you might say, my rite of passage. However, even though she let go of my hand, she would follow half a block behind me, until I entered the school building. She must have studied surveillance at Quantico, because it was impossible for me to shake her tail. I would dart into a drugstore and slip out the back door. And there she would be, reminding me to brush my teeth after lunch. I even tried wearing a false moustache as a disguise. Eventually, I accepted the fact that she was keeping an eye on me from a distance. It wasn't the perfect arrangement, but it was an improvement. At least she stopped sitting next to me in class.

I'm sure those of you who have a working mother and nine siblings would relish this kind of attention. However, for an only child it is embarrassing and onerous. To this day, I have a constant feeling that my mother is still following me. So, I generally travel under an assumed name.

Attending public school was one of the most enlightening experiences of my life. If I had attended Horace Mann, Fieldstone or one of the other elitist New York private schools, I would still be a Mama's boy today. Of course, I would also be able to read and write. But public school gave me a new perspective of the world. That of looking up while flat on my back. I was beat up more than an egg white in a zabaglione.

It was Guido Buttera who gave me my first bloody nose. It wasn't a bad way to lose my pugilistic virginity. All my other friends had suffered a bloody nose at one time or another. Herbie ran into a lamppost while playing stickball. Jay got in the way of Jennifer Lambert's wayward elbow. Now that was embarrassing. But, none of that kid stuff pour moi. I got my bloody nose from the King of Bloody Nose Givers, the Italian Stallion, Guido Buttera. The guy liked to beat people up more than he liked to steal hubcaps. He was so proficient at it he didn't even bother to start a fight first. He would just walk up to some unsuspecting classmate and ask "What did you say?" Then, before the poor kid could respond, WHAM! Right in the kisser. And, Guido was proud of it too. He had notches tattooed on his wrist. The good news was once you were beaten up by Guido he left you alone. It was a big school and he had to move quickly to initiate everyone. The most he might do to you later was establish his territory by peeing on your desk.

The worst part of my bloody nose was not the physical pain, but my mother's reaction. I came home from school early with blood on my shirt and huge cotton swabs protruding from my nostrils.

She took one look at me and screamed, "Oh my God! You tried to cross Amsterdam Avenue alone." I told her what had transpired and she hit the roof.

"As soon as I get you cleaned up, we are going to speak to the principal. Nobody can treat my son like this," she shouted.

"No, Mom." I lied. "It was an accident. He was aiming at the girl in front of me and she ducked. He didn't mean it, really."

She didn't buy it. She took me straight away to the principal's office where I proceeded to rat on Guido Buttera. As we sat in the principal's office, I saw my whole life flash in front of me. I had the distinct vision of my brains being crushed into manicotti by an Italian headlock. The principal assured my mother he would reprimand Guido. In other words, sign my death warrant. Every day after that I went to school and waited for the other shoe to drop—on my testicles. Nothing happened. Either the principal was smart enough to recognize my predicament, or else he didn't want to get a bloody nose.

Eventually, I learned, as did many of my Jewish peers, that I was a better talker than I was a fighter. This probably accounts for why there are more good Jewish lawyers than Jewish karate teachers. I developed an uncanny ability to talk my way out of anything. However, it didn't work too well at P.S. 87

because most of the students didn't understand English. So, I had to learn to do like my Yankee hero, Phil Rizutto, hit and run. I switch hit from being a fast talker to becoming a fast runner. I would run rings around the class bully. I had to. I wasn't allowed to cross Amsterdam Avenue alone.

There was a particular group of Puerto Rican students who formed a gang called the Warlords. These were macho tough hombres. I can't begin to tell you how many boloney sandwiches I paid in protection. Finally, in desperation, I formed my own gang of Jewish students to protect our lunches. We called ourselves the Landlords. There were quite a few territorial disputes between the rival gangs before we were able to put them out of business by doubling their rent.

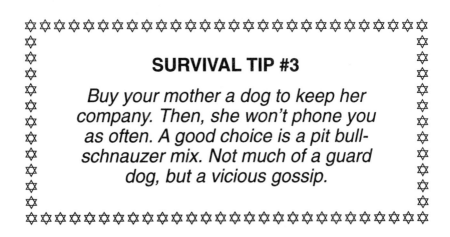

SURVIVAL TIP #3

Buy your mother a dog to keep her company. Then, she won't phone you as often. A good choice is a pit bull-schnauzer mix. Not much of a guard dog, but a vicious gossip.

CHAPTER 9

THE CALAMINE LOTION KID

Once I had traversed Amsterdam Avenue alone, I was ready to go out on my own. My friend Herbie had attended Camp Wanatonga in Maine for the past two summers. He told me of all the fun times he had having pillow fights and playing baseball with the other guys. And, of the nights spent in front of the campfire roasting marshmellows and listening to scary tales. Boy. It sounded super. I asked my folks if I could go to camp with Herbie the next summer.

My mother did not take my request well. "Don't you know there are big bears in the Maine woods," she told me. "Did you forget what happened to Gertrude Gittleman's son at camp last summer. He almost drowned."

This was a difficult argument to overcome, even though Bernie Gittleman was in the bathtub at the time of the incident in question. But, I really wanted to go to camp. It was time to take affirmative action. So I went to my father. He had been a counselor at camp as a teenager and was on my side.

After a long conversation between my folks, it was decided. I could attend camp next summer. However, Camp Wanatonga was out of the question. For one thing, Maine was too far from New York City. Second, it was an all boys camp, and too rough and tumble. Instead, my parents selected the co-ed Camp Summerset in the nearby Catskills. They thought it was a safe place. The camp had showers, not bathtubs.

There I was, eight years old and waiving goodbye to my folks as the train slowly pulled away from Grand Central Station. I was so excited I could hardly breathe. However, as the train passed 125th Street reality set in. I wasn't near my mother. In fact, every minute I was moving further away. By the time the train hit the North Bronx, I was hopelessly homesick. And, when it rolled passed Larchmont, I wanted out. I think I would have pulled the emergency stop handle by Scarsdale, except for feeling guilty. After all the time my mother spent sewing all those little nametags in my socks, the least I could do was give camp a try.

To my way of thinking, the time spent on those nametags was an effort in futility. After all the socks which were lost in the washer at home, I didn't see how giving them an identity would be of any help. Maybe, if she had just sewn in a phone number it would be better. That way if the socks got lost, they could call home. Disappearing socks is one of the true mysteries of life. I still wonder where they all go. Probably to the same place as Jimmy Hoffa's socks went. Unfortunately for Hoffa, he was in his when they disappeared.

Camp Summerset was not what I expected. The girls outnumbered the boys two to one. And, the boys weren't very macho. Maybe it was because the camp colors were pink and mauve. The big sport was tether-ball, a game in which you attempt to entwine a volleyball on a string around a pole before your opponent does. For those of you who have never had the opportunity to play tether-ball, you don't know what you are missing. It is as exciting as pic-up-sticks, but not quite as fast paced. I became very adept at tether-ball. If it ever becomes an Olympic sport, I'm a shoe-in for the team.

Another popular sport played at Summerset was "immies," also known as marbles to less sophisticated readers. It took a keen eye and steady hand to hit and capture an opponents "purees," the more valuable cloudless marbles. The important thing was to make sure your adversary didn't cheat and kept her knuckle on the ground when she shot. By the end of my first week at camp, I had collected a sock full of purees. I would have had a lot more, but I lost my other sock.

The most popular activity at Camp Summerset were the nature walks. The idea was to run through the pine forest to see who could fall on poison sumac first. I don't mean to brag, but they nicknamed me the "Calamine Lotion Kid."

Since the boys and girls shared activities, the camp frowned on contact sports. Even softball and flag football were taboo. The Camp Director was ahead of his time. He was being cautious years before negligence suits became fashionable. But, I was getting bored silly with horseshoes and badminton. If they sang

"This is Table Number One" again I was ready to throw up. Even playing solo boomerang was more fun.

Every day I would write my mother the same post card. "They have put in bathtubs. Get me out of here." I didn't know my counselor was reading my mail until one day he cancelled my canteen privileges. I couldn't buy any more stamps.

Finally, after three weeks of roasting marshmellows, Parents Weekend arrived. I was never so happy to see two people in my entire life. I recognized them immediately. And, they recognized I was suffering from a severe case of homesickness. Yet, they were torn between letting me come home, and forcing me to become more independent. They decided to compromise. I would have to stay at Camp Summerset; however, my mother would join me. She stayed at the camp director's home at night and spent the days with me. This was not exactly the solution I had in mind, but it did give us a decided advantage during color war. The Pinks ran the Mauves silly.

At my mother's insistence, I gave Camp Summerset another try the following summer. In truth, it worked out much better. I probably would have lasted the whole summer if I wasn't asked to leave when they caught my mother cheating at marbles.

CHAPTER 10

TRADITION!
JEWISH KRAZY GLUE

As Tevye, the Milkman, in Fiddler on the Roof, put it, "Because of our traditions, everyone knows who he is and what God expects of him. Without traditions, our life would be as shaky as a Fiddler on the Roof." This probably accounts for why so many Jews suffer from shingles.

Customs, rituals, ethics and values combine to give the Jewish people a unique identity. Because Jews have suffered so much oppression throughout the centuries, a Jewish mother feels an obligation to instill this identity upon her children from day one. This is usually accomplished by providing her offspring with a larger than average nose.

Thereafter, youngsters begin to appreciate their Jewish heritage by what they experience at home. My mother began my religious education by telling me bedtime stories about Jewish history. I particularly remember the story of Hanukah. She explained it was the celebration of the survival of Judaism dating back to 200 B.C. During that period, King Antiochus of Syria attempted to unify his empire by insisting that all his subjects adopt one religion based on the worship of the God Zeus. This didn't sit too well with the Jews in

Syria who thought Zeus was full of hot air. They insisted on following the mandates of the Torah. Antiochus decreed the Jews must abandon their faith and publicly embrace paganism or face execution.

The plot thickened when a group of Jews, led by Judah Maccabee, refused to accept the King's dictate. Although significantly outnumbered by the King's forces, the valiant band used guerrilla warfare to retake the Temple in Jerusalem and secure their religious freedom. Mom explained that this one event became the basis for both Sylvester Stallone's Rocky and Rambo series. However, the movie shoot locations were changed to Philadelphia and Vietnam because the Temple in Jerusalem was already booked for the Kidderman Bar Mitzvah.

Another Jewish holiday I remember fondly is Passover, which commemorates the Jewish Exodus from Egypt. A ceremonial "seder" or pig-out is the gastronomical denouement of the holiday. It is called a pig-out because Jews do not eat pork.

It is customary for everyone at the seder to drink four cups of wine, including the children. When it came time for me to fulfill my responsibility as the youngest child to ask the traditional "Four Questions," I could only think of one, "Where is the bathroom?" Later in the evening, it was my job to open the front door for the prophet Elijah. By the time I staggered over, fumbled with the knob, and finally opened it, he had already left.

Rosh Hashannah, the Jewish New Year, was

another holiday I truly enjoyed. Unlike the secular New Year celebrated by us all, Rosh Hashannah falls on different days each year. However, because of an elaborate warning system, a Jew really can't miss its approach. A hollowed out ram's horn, called a "shofer," is blown every weekday morning during the month immediately preceding the High Holy Days. The shrill noise always reminded my mother to make New Year's Eve dinner reservations.

A recurring theme pervaded the stories of Jewish history my mother told to me. We were a persecuted people. Stories of the Exodus from Egypt, the Spanish Inquisition, the Czarist Pogroms, and restricted country clubs brought the point home clearly.

One might imagine living as a persecuted people would be a terrible burden. Yet, according to my mother, nothing could be further from the truth. She admitted that a persecution complex can be quite a (excuse the expression) cross to bear. But, she maintained that Jews do not suffer from persecution complexes. That malady is for people who only think they are being persecuted. The Jews know they are being persecuted. As my mother explained it, Jews are persecuted because others are jealous of their intelligence and ambition. Adeptly, she had wisely turned a persecution complex into a superiority complex. She considered this to be a much healthier mania.

She even had evidence that a "yiddishe kup" is intellectually superior to a "goyishe kup." Statistics she had compiled showed American Jews twice as likely to attend college as non-Jews. And, three times as likely to attend graduate school. Furthermore, Jewish women are six times as likely to marry a doctor.

This data may be related to natural intelligence, but more probably to the serious emphasis Jewish mothers place on education and success. My birth announcement is a case in point. It read, in part, "We are proud to announce the birth of our son, the doctor, on March 15, 1938."

The following example will further emphasize this point. Given that there is one Jew for every three hundred people in the world, a Jew should win the Nobel Prize once every thirty years. However, so many Jews have won the Nobel Prize that there has been talk of changing the name to the Nobel Naches. So great is the Jewish monopoly that if, in a given year, a Jew does not win, they suspect the Swedes of Anti-Semitism.

As made clear in the fable of David and Goliath, a Jew must think quickly and never leave a stone unturned. The trick in dealing with persecution lies in how a Jew defines the word. The Jewish scholar and linguist, Dr. R. Ticulate, defines persecution as "the act of harassing someone because he is more intelligent and ambitious." Consequently, in spite of the difficulties they have encountered over the centuries, Jews feel proud of being a persecuted people.

Contrast this position with African-Americans who feel that they have been unfairly persecuted because others think they are inferior. These different interpretations of persecution explain why it is easier for a Jew to become a member of a restricted country club than it is for an African-American. An African-American would have to soak for days in a bath of Clorox and be exorcized of rhythm. A Jew, on the other hand, has only to change his name, get a nose job, cross himself before taking a foul shot and develop a drinking problem.

SURVIVAL TIP #4

When you go on vacation, give your mother a contact telephone number with a few digits transposed. This way she won't think you are trying to avoid her, yet she won't be able to bother you.

Eg: Mother: "Oy, I'm so glad I reached you. I was so worried you didn't call."

Son: "Don't worry. I'm a big boy. I can take care of myself."

Mother: "So you say. But remember the time you didn't wear your gloves and you caught a bad cold."

Son: "That was years ago."

Mother: "So what. You were in the Minneapolis City Hospital for a week. We worried that you had caught pneumonia."

Son: "Minneapolis? I've never been in Minneapolis."

Mother: "Oy, I must have the wrong number. Anyway young man, you should take better care of yourself."

CHAPTER 11

FROM BOYHOOD TO MANHOOD FASTER THAN YOU CAN SAY, "PASS THE CHOPPED LIVER."

Nothing is more steeped in Jewish tradition than the Bar Mitzvah ceremony. This is the time in the cycle of life when the Jewish boy reaches the age of thirteen and is considered a man. Many primitive cultures celebrate a young man's thirteenth birthday as the time he reaches puberty. The celebrations differ in, at least, one respect. Jewish youngsters eat chopped chicken liver while the others eat alligator, which they have to catch barehanded and bare naked. The naked part is easy as not many alligators dress up. So, as rites of passage go, the Bar Mitzvah is not a bad alternative. It is not, however, a slam dunk.

For one thing, the Bar Mitzvah boy has to read from the Torah. The Torah is filled with a bunch of words that look like a cross between hieroglyphics and a bad musical score. In fact, these words have no recognizable letters whatsoever. There were more characters on one page of the Torah than on my entire family tree. To make it more confusing, you have to read it backwards. It is easier for a blind man to solve a

Rubix Cube puzzle than for a youngster to learn Hebrew.

There is, however, some consolation for a Jewish youngster who is forced to learn Hebrew. He doesn't have to remember a word of it once the ceremony is over. In future synagogue services, all he has to do during prayer is lipsinc the rabbi. Lipsincing a cantor is a bit more difficult. Many of them have black beards which cover their lips. Our cantor, who's first name was Eddie, had a wonderful personality but his voice was a bit suspect. When he told my mother he had insured his voice for $100,000, she responded, "Well, I hope you invested the proceeds wisely."

It is interesting to note that even though the Torah is read during the ceremony, Bar Mitzvahs are not mentioned in the holy book. This is because the Bar Mitzvah ceremony did not even exist until the fourteenth century. This also explains why we have never seen a picture of Jesus Christ wearing a blue serge suit.

Not only must the Bar Mitzvah boy read from the Torah in Hebrew, but he must also give a speech in English to an audience of friends and relatives. It is tradition that the speech begins with the words, "Today I am a man," and goes on to thank his parents for all they have done for him. I had prepared my speech for days and read it over several hundred times. However, when it came time for me to deliver it, I froze. As I looked at the myriad of smiling faces staring up at me, all I could think was, "I've never seen any of these people in my entire life. Either my folks had invited every distant relative they could find, or I'm at the wrong Bar Mitzvah." I was about to panic until I saw a familiar face. Seated in the third row was Guido Buttera, the schoolyard bully. He was pointing a finger at me and saying "What did you say!"

As it turned out, my mother had invited every distant relative she could find. In fact, the more distant the better. Some from as far away as Kiev. Mom figured they wouldn't come, but would still send a present. As usual, she was absolutely correct. Most of them sent me $50 Savings Bonds. Unfortunately, they had been issued by The Republic of Bangladesh. Those who didn't send savings bonds sent fountain pens. Although they came in a bevy of shapes and colors, the pens shared a common trait. They all leaked. That's probably why they are called "fountain" pens. The most useful gift I received was from Uncle Lenny. He gave me a blotter.

As is tradition, my father presented me with a "phylacteries," or "tefillin", a morning prayer shawl. Placing the strings of the tefillin on my arm, dad shook my hand and said, "Congratulations son, today you are a man." The tefillin kept sliding off. It wasn't till years later someone got the idea to put it on pots and pans. Mom picked up the tefillin and pinned it to my jacket. She gave me a huge hug and added these reassuring words. "You'll always be my little boychik."

The most impressive thing about a Bar Mitzvah is not the ceremony, but the feast that follows. By Jewish standards, I had a rather moderate gathering of 600 of our relatives, mom's canasta partners and dad's business associates at the Sherry Netherlands Hotel on Fifth Avenue. There was an awe-inspiring buffet of the most delicious foods imaginable. Latke, lox mit cream cheese and bagel, blintz, gefilta fish, borsht, kreplach, kugelflanken, stuffed derma, chopped chicken liver mit shmaltz. All of these foods are highly recommended in the best selling book "Final Exit." Champagne and liquor flowed like my fountain pens. There were two bands playing—simultaneously. Cantor Eddie sang a resounding rendition of "Hava Negila." Many thought he was imitating Eartha Kitt.

My mother was as proud as I have ever seen her. She kept repeating, "Look at my little boy, the big man."

CHAPTER 12

CONQUERING SEX SINGLE-HANDEDLY

Puberty brought many things to hand, so to speak. Whenever I tried to discuss the birds and bees with my mother, she would say, "Ask your father—the sex maniac." Consequently, my sexual development became a catalyst for cultivating a relationship with my father.

As you have probably noticed by now, I have said relatively little about my father. This is because I never saw him as a child. He was already an adult when we met. Nor did I see him very much when I was a child. As is the case in most Jewish homes, my mother was responsible for my upbringing. Dad would throw out an occasional word of wisdom, such as "Listen to your mother!" They made a great team. She laid down the law and he enforced it. My father believed in fair and equal punishment. He could spank me with either hand.

My mother told me she fell in love with my father the first day she laid eyes on him. He was terribly shy. It took him three months before he had the nerve to ask her out on a date. He saved up so he could take her to the fanciest restaurant he knew.

"He was such a gentleman," my mother reminisced, "He insisted on busing my tray."

My dad did not come from a wealthy family and had to work very hard to support us. He was in the rag business and traveled during the week. One week he would be "shlepping" dresses to Philadelphia and Washington. The next week to Chicago and Milwaukee. It would have been easier to simply carry the dresses, but he was Jewish, and Jews shlep. It takes a lot more effort to shlep than carry, but when it's over you feel better about yourself. Unfortunately, you are too exhausted to care.

My father actually shlepped and slept thru my childhood. On Friday, he would return from his trip. I would be so happy to see him. But, he was always so exhausted he would have dinner and then fall asleep. He would sleep through the weekend and be on the road again Monday morning. Like so many of the American Jewish males of his generation, he was a workaholic and proud of it.

Jewish men in the '40s had a different mind set than today. They had lived through the Great Depression and insecurity abounded. Committed to never going hungry again, they put every waking hour into making enough money to save for the inevitable rainy day. Dad was a perceptive businessman. He outguessed the depression by going bankrupt two years earlier.

In spite of my father's absence, my mother had a way of using it to advantage. If I disobeyed her, she would say, "Just you wait until your father comes home," or "Wait till I tell your father what you did." I would dread the approach of the weekend. But, by the time dad returned home, my mother always forgot to tell him of my transgression. He probably wouldn't have punished me anyway since he didn't walk in his sleep.

The only real heart to heart discussions I can remember having with my father revolved around sex. However, he was quite shy about discussing the subject with me. His usual answer was, "I'll tell you when you are older." Sometimes he would put me off with, "You'll find out soon enough." This was particularly frustrating for someone who was planning on growing up to be a gynecologist. I felt I was in the "need to know" category.

In truth, my dad was a master of misinformation about sex. For example, there was the time he got angry at me for spending too much time in the bathroom. We had just one bathroom in our apartment and it was the only room with a lock on the door. Somehow, sitting on the throne with the door locked gave me a sense of privacy I relished. Dad seemed to think I was relishing more than my privacy. He would yell through the bathroom door, "I'm warning you. If you don't stop doing that so much, you'll go blind." I had no idea what he was referring to. Now, every time I suffer from constipation, I visit an ophthalmologist.

One of the early ways I learned about sex was to listen in at my parent's bedroom door at night. For a long time, I thought that having a headache was a kind of foreplay. On a few occasions, I would hear my dad breathing heavily. I thought he was quite a passionate lover. Later, I found out he suffered from asthma. When my dad would sigh, "Oh Baby, Oh Baby," Mom would counter with, "Your hands are freezing," or something equally endearing.

I wasn't sure whether my folks had a good sex life or not. I only know my dad had a strobe light installed over their bed so that when they made love it appeared my mother was moving.

Most of my early sex education came, not from my parents, but from my junior high school classmates. I would be regaled by the conquests of my buddies. Herbie got to first base with Jessica on a blind date. Seth actually got bare tit from Sally. Everyone was a Don Juan but me. It was quite humiliating.

Finally, I got an idea. I made up an imaginary girlfriend. I named her Maureen. Boy, was she hot. Suddenly, I had some great locker room stories to tell my cronies. I paced myself well. First date, we talked for hours and really hit it off. Second date, I kissed her goodnight. Third date, we did some heavy petting. By the fourth date, I was getting pretty excited myself. Making up romantic stories was easy for me. The difficult part was giving myself hickies on the neck.

One day my mother got a detailed description of my adventures from Herbie's mom. She confronted me and I was too embarrassed to tell her the truth.

"You have a girlfriend, at your age." she said incredulously, "What's her name?"

"Maureen O'Hara," I responded. It was the first

name to come to mind. Probably because I had just seen her in "The Spanish Main" and was smitten by her flaming red hair. As names go, it was not a good choice.

"O'Hara," my mother responded, "This is not a Jewish name."

What followed was a long dissertation on why it was important for me to date Jewish girls. My mind was only half listening. The other half was making it with Maureen O'Hara. My mother's logic didn't stand a chance.

Following this incident, my mother decided it was time to introduce me to some "nice" Jewish girls. So, she signed me up to take dance lessons at the Viola Wolfe Studio. It consisted of a series of eight weekly sessions with a number of other thirteen year olds, divided equally between the sexes. This turned out to be one of the most embarrassing experiences of my young life.

All the boys had to dress in suits and ties and wear white gloves. We were taught to go over to a girl, formally introduce ourselves, and ask her if she would like to dance. Most of these girls had matured quicker than their male counterparts. None of them had flaming red hair, but they made up for it by all being about a foot taller than I was. That put my head about shoulder level when we were dancing. In the case of one of the more developed young ladies, my head was even lower. And, that's when I first realized a part of my anatomy had a mind of its own. Trying to sound romantic, I got up on my tiptoes and whispered in her ear, "Your hands are freezing." She responded by slapping my face.

Not wanting to be denied, I approached a pretty girl standing alone. She had a cigarette in her mouth. I went over and suavely lit it. Just like I had seen Humphry Bogart do in the movies. She got pretty angry when all the chocolate melted on her new white dress.

When I got home, I was so frustrated that I locked myself in the bathroom. At least there I could have sex with someone who understood me.

SURVIVAL TIP #5

If you are dating a non-Jew, give him a few words of Yiddish to spread around in conversation with your mother. That way, she won't give you the third degree.

Eg: Daughter: "Mom, I'd like you to meet my friend, Sammy."

Sammy: "A real pleasure to meet you, Mrs. Finkelstein. Your daughter is lovely. She must give you a lot of naches."

Mother: "She certainly does."

Sammy: "Oy, look at the time. I have to get home for dinner. My mother is making my favorite dish, kreplach."

Mother: (to daughter, after Sammy leaves) "What a haymisha young man. What did you say his name was?"

Daughter: "Sammy. Sammy Wong."

CHAPTER 13

THIS CHAPTER WAS SKIPPED BECAUSE MY MOTHER IS SUPERSTITIOUS.

CHAPTER 14

COLLEGE BOUND
AND GAGGED

One of the most traumatic periods in a Jewish mother's life is when her son or daughter leaves home to go to college. Although education is paramount to a Jewish mother, the thought of her child being away is almost too much to bear.

My mother was quite excited when I told her I wanted to have a college education. She immediately sent away for every home-study course catalogue she could locate. After reading all of the curriculums carefully, she was particularly impressed with Hooked on Phonics. She recommended it highly in spite of the fact I would have to leave home for the final exam, which was given at the local public library.

She was dumbstruck when I chose to go to Brown University, even though Providence was only a three hour train ride from New York. She accompanied me to the campus for my interview with the Dean of Admissions, and we did quite well. She answered all the questions directed at me glibly and confidently. The dean was so impressed that he enrolled her immediately. I was put on the waiting list.

I remember that first day I left for college. My mother insisted I wear my dad's old raccoon coat so I wouldn't catch cold. This was a little disconcerting since we were in the midst of an Indian summer. Actually, the coat came in handy during football games and for hiding when my Aunt Beckie came to visit. I shook hands goodbye with my dad, and my mother gave me a big hug. Then she uttered the words that would permeate my college career, "Don't forget to call home."

When I arrived at Brown, I was placed in a dormitory room with two other Jewish freshman. This would have been fine except we only shared one telephone. We kept arguing who's mother not to call first. One of my roommates, Billy Vogel, played the tuba. With football season approaching, he was constantly practicing for the marching band. My other roommate, Lew Krieger, was trying out for the cheerleader squad. Every evening from 7 to 10 we had a half time show in our room. It was impossible to study. I kept getting hit on the head by an errant baton. One day, totally frustrated, I decided to hide Billy's tuba. I spent an hour looking for a spot large enough to hide it. I was about ready to give up until I spotted my dad's raccoon coat.

Since I was now a collegian, my mother no longer called me "boychick." I was now "Mr. Smartie Pants," particularly when I would forget to call home. Every time I would call, I would get the same rhetorical question. "So, Mr Smartie Pants, how come you never call home." And that was from the AT&T operator. It didn't matter how often I called, it was never often enough. As soon as my mother heard my voice, she

CHAPTER 15

JEWS DON'T PLAY WITH PIGSKINS

Y ou may wonder why there are no Jewish football players. Where are the Bo Ginsbergs and the Bubba Horowitzs hiding. The answer is that Jews do not do contact sports. Yes, there have been a few Jewish sports stars over the years such as Hank Greenberg, Al Rosen, Max Zaslofsky, and Lew Alcindor. But, for the most part, Jews have chosen to own teams rather than play on them. This is because ringing in every Jew's ears are the words of his mother, "Watch out! You are going to hurt yourself doing that."

I really wanted to play football in college. I was fast, fairly strong, and highly competitive. However, when my mother found out I was trying out for the Freshman team, she went ballistic. Her frantic phone call brought me back to reality.

"Are you out of your mind?" she asked. "Do you think your father spent $2,000 on your braces so you could lose your teeth playing some dumb game? Is that what you think we are paying all that money to send you to college for?"

Jewish mothers are the consummate experts of the rhetorical question. If I had a dollar for every sentence my mother finished with a question mark, I could afford to buy my own pro team. The true power of the rhetorical question comes not in the question itself, but rather its intonation and phraseology. Let's analyze my mother's statement. First, "Are you out of your mind?" Immediately you are put on the defensive. There is only one answer, "No, but..." Then comes the setup. "Do you think your father spent $2,000 so you could lose your teeth playing some dumb game." There are three distinct parts to this statement, one more devastating than the next. The obvious one is guilt and that alone will do the trick. How can you ignore all the money your family sacrificed so you won't wind up looking like Rodney King. Add to that the not so subtle hint that you are going to get all your teeth knocked out. This lends a certain anxiety to the feeling of guilt. Finally, the fact that you are risking everything playing some "dumb game." Not only are you guilty and anxious, but you are stupid to boot. And all this is bundled up in one rhetorical question.

Then comes the coup de gras, "Is that what you think we are paying all that money to send you to college for?" As is the case with all Jewish children, I was no match for my mother's eloquence. However, I was able to convince her to let me go to the first week of "non-contact" practice. It was an interesting week for me. Every afternoon after class, I would don my uniform and rush out to the practice field. On the sidelines stood my mother and our personal physician. After every play, he would give me a complete physical. It was not easy for him to get the fluoroscope machine under my shoulder pads.

Our first game was against Dartmouth University. My mother was a nervous wreck. Fortunately for her, I didn't play in the game. Every time the coach sent me in the game, we would be penalized for having too many players on the field. It was probably because my mother was holding my hand. Even though I didn't play, my mother, a great believer in preventative medicine, sent me to the Mayo Clinic for a three day evaluation.

Our second game was a non-Ivy League contest against a rough Rhode Island University squad. This team was so tough they had a Consiglione as their mascot. Every player looked and acted like Guido Buttera. This was probably due to the fact that he was the team's captain. Yet, as tough as Guido was, the most intimidating player on the team was Buzzer Bednarick. The 220 pound linebacker was so powerful and speedy that he could knock an opponent flat and pick his pocket at the same time. Nobody knew how old Buzzer really was. After retiring from the Army, he enrolled in RIU and had captained the team for the past nine years. The Rhode Island Wreckers had developed a vaunted reputation for their "Pancake Defense." A simple alignment in which one player would clip an opponent from behind and the other ten would jump on the fallen foe, preferably cleats first. Occasionally, they would even do this to the ball carrier.

It was my first starting assignment and I was stoked. We won the toss and elected to receive. "Goodie Two Shoes" Goodman, our fleet return specialist, brought the ball back to our own seven yard line. After he was carried off the field, we went into the huddle. From between my legs I could see Guido Buttera jumping up and down and pointing a finger in my direction. I was hoping he didn't recognize me. Then I heard him yelling, "What did you say! What did you say!" But, his voice was overshadowed by that of my mother, who was in the huddle calling for a quick kick.

What most people don't know is that football was not always a non- Jewish sport. In the mid 1930s, Yeshiva University did have a Varsity football team. In the three years they operated, the team compiled a 1-34 won-lost record. The only game they were victorious in was an inter-faith contest against Our Sisters of the Sacred Heart. The Sisters were leading by three points with less than a minute to play and had possession of the ball on their own 10 yard line. The situation looked extremely bleak for the Yeshiva Yutzs even though they were certain to beat the point spread. But, that day God proved we were the Chosen People. On a bootleg play, the Sacred Heart quarterback, Sister Dion, fumbled the ball in her own end zone. She appeared to recover the fumble and a huge pileup followed. When the players were untangled, lying at the bottom of the pile was our defensive tackle, Big Ben Chutzpah, with the ball in his arms. It was a touchdown and Yeshiva won the game. Later Big Ben explained how he had recovered the ball. "It was easy once I got into the habit," he bragged.

Excited by the team's victory, Rabbi Morris Schwartzman, President of Yeshiva, decided to institute a serious recruiting program for the next season. He traveled the United States looking for talented Jewish high school football players. He was successful in recruiting three blue chip offensive linemen from the same small Texas high school, beating out Notre Dame by only a few dollars. Unfortunately, the three never reported to the opening day of school. Two of the boys failed their final exam in calf wrestling. The third joined the Klu Klux Klan. He was, however, expelled after only a few gatherings because his nose kept protruding from the sheet.

Frustrated by his failure to find quality Jewish athletes, President Schwartzman decided to abolish football at the university. "Jews don't play with pigskins." he explained to a disappointed alumni.

My college football career came to an abrupt end when I got the wind knocked out of me while attempting to recover a fumble against Yale.

My mother refused to let me play after that. She said she was acting under her lawyer's advice. Two weeks later, she filed a lawsuit against the Yale University football team for unnecessary roughness.

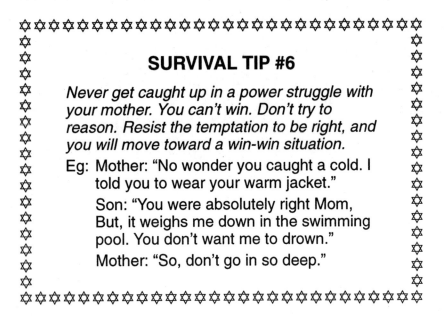

SURVIVAL TIP #6

Never get caught up in a power struggle with your mother. You can't win. Don't try to reason. Resist the temptation to be right, and you will move toward a win-win situation.

Eg: Mother: "No wonder you caught a cold. I told you to wear your warm jacket."

Son: "You were absolutely right Mom, But, it weighs me down in the swimming pool. You don't want me to drown."

Mother: "So, don't go in so deep."

CHAPTER 16

MY SON THE LAWYER

It is crucial to every Jewish mother that her son become a professional and that her daughter marry one. A child who is a successful professional gives the Jewish mother two huge benefits. First, she can get free professional advice. Second, and more important, she can give free professional advice. As if by osmosis, she automatically becomes an expert in her child's chosen profession.

When I decided not to become a doctor, my mother was truly disappointed. Reluctantly, she took down the "Doctor Is In" shingle hanging on the front door of our apartment, and wondered what she was going to do with the box of blank prescription pads she had just ordered. However, when I told her I was going to go to law school she perked up. She immediately phoned her friend, Gertrude, who was having marital problems.

"Stay with the schlemiel another three years," she told her friend. "And Stevie will get you a divorce settlement you wouldn't believe."

Becoming a lawyer was not my first choice for a career. I had the entrepreneurial spirit, and wanted to be an instantaneous success. Three years of law school, and who knows how many more apprenticing, seemed like an eternity. However, my friend Jay had just gone broke on a business venture and I was not willing to take the same risk with my business idea.

Jay had been training carrier pigeons on his roof top. He had the idea of sending mail overnight long before Federal Express was ever started. For a while, everything went well with his letter delivery service. However, when he introduced his "two pounds for two dollars" service, he lost his entire fleet. The added weight caused the pigeons to plummet to the sidewalk.

"Didn't I tell you it was a fly by night operation," Jay's mother told him.

My entrepreneurial concept was quite different from Jay's. I had the idea of setting up drive-thru psychoanalysis kiosks all over town. The driver would pull up to a talking dummy, kind of like Jack In The Box but with a goatee and bifocals. He would explain his problem and get a quick fix from the psychologist in the box. For an extra buck, he could order a BLT to go. I was going to franchise the concept under the name Mc Therapy. I thought this would have a big appeal in the Jewish community, particularly if I offered a two-for-one guilt therapy session on Tuesdays. I had a similar idea of a drive-thru confessional for Catholics on the run. I was going to call it Mc Penance. But, as I said earlier, I chickened out and went on to Columbia Law School.

My mother was delighted I chose Columbia. I could live at home and commute to classes. This would give her the opportunity to help me with my homework so she could bone up on her new career. She worked with me on all of my homework assignments, but the results really didn't show until the day of " moot court." Moot court is where the law student presents a case before a real judge. These judges can be very intimidating, asking pertinent and difficult questions. When it came time to give my presentation, the judge asked me "Why do you think the Plaintiff should get relief?" To which I answered "So, why Not?" After that incident I thought it would be best to do my homework alone.

My graduation from law school was a particularly exciting day for my mother. She sent out invitations to everyone she knew, including our relatives in Kiev. For a month prior to the graduation, she chased ambulances and placed invitations in the pockets of numerous unconscious pedestrians. She even took out an ad in the New York Times. It read "My son, Stevie, is graduating from Columbia Law School this Saturday. Everyone is welcome, particularly if you are suffering from whiplash."

Thanks to my mother's efforts, I was visited by almost every member of our family after I began work at a midtown Manhattan law firm. It seems each of my relatives had a legal problem which they had nursed for years until I had graduated. Aunt Beckie was the first to arrive, with a huge cast on her left arm.

"What happened to you?" I asked with concern.

"I think my arm is broken," she responded. "I was walking in Bloomingdale's right after the janitor had washed the floor. The yutz forgot to put out the "Wet

Floor" sign and I fell flat on my face. Do you think I have a case?"

"I certainly do," I said. "When did this happen?"

"Six years ago," she answered. "But it's really starting to hurt now."

Following Aunt Beckie into my office was her husband, my uncle Dave. He wanted to sue Bloomingdale's for loss of consortium. It seems Aunt Beckie hadn't slept with him since he canceled her Bloomingdale's charge card.

Uncle Morris wanted to sue his wife . Apparently he had bought a Brazilian parrot at a pet store for $300. The proprietor assured him the parrot spoke more than twelve languages fluently. The next day when Morris returned from work, his wife Sadie had cooked the parrot for dinner.

"Are you out of your mind," he told his wife. "Didn't you know that parrot could speak twelve languages fluently."

"So, he should-a said something." she answered.

I even received a call from my mother's friend Gertrude. "I've stuck with this schlemiel for three years," she said. "It's time we took him for all he's worth."

When my relatives were not coming by or calling, my mother was. She wanted to know how each of my cases was going and gave me her legal advice without hesitation. She would call every day and insist she be put through to me even if I was on the phone with a client. Constantly, she gave me her opinion on how I should handle a legal matter. It was getting to be disturbing. What was even more disturbing was when the firm gave her a bigger Christmas bonus than they gave me.

Finally, in desperation, I decided to specialize in sports law. Since Jews are such lousy athletes I figured I wouldn't have to deal with my family. But, I wasn't in my new office for more than a day before my uncle Lenny dropped by. He wanted to file a negligence action against Willie Mays for getting picked off first base by Sandy Koufax during a crucial playoff game. Lenny had lost a twenty dollar bet on the contest and felt Mays should cover the wager.

CHAPTER 17

TO LOVE HONOR AND OH BOY!

My mother was always trying to fix me up with one of her friend's daughters. I had more blind dates than Stevie Wonder. She was secretly hoping I would marry Adelle Ginsberg, her friend Gertrude's daughter. Every time my parents had a party, Adelle was invited. She usually showed up wearing a wedding gown. There was nothing wrong with Adelle that a talented team of plastic surgeons couldn't fix. Of course, one of them would have to be an expert in liposuction as well. Adelle was so fat that after riding on a merry go round, the carousel horse limped.

Edna Finkel was another of my mother's choices. I should have gotten the message when she told me Edna was a "nice girl." This was another way of saying she came from a wealthy Jewish family. She was so ugly as a kid that her parents hired the next door neighbor's little girl to take Edna's place in their family photographs. All my mother's choices were fixer uppers.

Ironically, as much effort as a Jewish mother puts forth in fixing up her child, she is always shocked when they decide to get married. It is particularly exasperating when it is a son who is about to tie the proverbial knot. She suddenly looks upon her future daughter-in-law as competition for her son's time and affection.

When I told my mother I was getting married, she immediately went off to fix up the guest room. I explained we wanted our own home, but it didn't sink in. She insisted we live in the apartment and even offered to take the surveillance camera out of my bedroom. When we refused, she forced me to sign a pre-nuptial agreement. It said in the event I got a divorce, I would agree to move back home.

In anticipation of that day, my mother kept my bedroom exactly as it was before I left. She even placed a mannequin in my bed so she wouldn't miss me too much. She took the mannequin's temperature twice a night. Once she even called the doctor because the dummy looked "exceedingly pale."

I'll never forget the day I told my mother I had gotten engaged.

"I'm shocked," she said. "I've got to call Gertrude and give her the good news."

When I explained it was not Adelle Ginsberg I was going to marry, but Samantha Smith, my mother looked concerned.

"Smith doesn't sound Jewish to me." she said with trepidation.

"No mom," I answered with embarrassment.

"She's not Jewish, but I love her very much."

"You're marrying a shiksa!" she screamed, then added calmly, "Excuse me for just a moment, I have to go to the bathroom."

After the doctor arrived and pumped her stomach, she continued the conversation.

"Mixed marriages are like tornadoes. After all the blowing and sucking stops, you lose your house," she counseled.

My mother was a lifetime member of the MMMMMM Club. No, it's not a gourmet society sponsored by Campbell Soup. MMMMMM stands for Mixed Marriages Make Most Mothers Miserable. Actually, it's less a club, than it is a fraternity. It doesn't have a lobby in Washington, or even an alcove. Membership is bestowed automatically on any Jewish mother who's child is about to marry a gentile. If the intended spouse has a different colored skin, the mother earns immediate Platinum status, and double points. Points can be redeemed for psychiatric visits.

The Club's motto is "Oy vay." You can tell a member by the way the "Oy" is pronounced. It is rolled out slowly by the tongue, followed by a sharp release of breath as though she was just punched in the stomach by Mike Tyson. Or, just found out he was her new son-in-law. The "vay" is anti-climatic, if the "Oy is properly presented.

The Club's secret salute, which accompanies the "Oy vay," is made by placing the palms of each hand over the ears, and shaking the head back and forth despairingly. Platinum members are entitled to add the words, "iz-mere," to the "Oy vay."

After taking the MMMMMM Club's 12-point program, my mother was much more resigned to my marriage. In fact, when it came to making the wedding plans, she jumped in with both high heels. Samantha's parents, Floyd and Rosie, wanted a small, intimate affair with close relatives and friends only. My mother, on the other hand, wanted to celebrate the event in the Waldorf Astoria's Grand Ballroom, capacity 2000. This created a slight bone of contention with the in-laws to be who were footing the bill. They wanted to serve chicken. My mother insisted on Beef Wellington. They wanted beer and wine only. Mom wanted Dom Perignon. Finally, after considerable bickering, a compromise was reached. Our side could invite as many guests as we wished, and Samantha's folks would keep all of the cover charge.

The next problem was agreeing on a date for the wedding. Samantha's folks wanted to have it on a Monday afternoon between 3 and 3:45 p.m. My mother wanted to have it during the entire month of August. When they couldn't agree, Samantha took the matter into her own hands.

"Enough of this bickering," she told me. "I want you to choose a date for our wedding."

"But, I don't want a date," I protested. "I want to go with you."

The wedding ceremony was held at Temple Beth El. At that time it was difficult to get a rabbi to work a mixed marriage. So, Samantha had to pretend she was Jewish. She wore thick eye glasses with a fake rubber nose attached. I looked over at her and a scary realization hit me. Our children were going to look like Woody Allen.

There we were, standing under the Huppah, the traditional canopy symbolizing the marital home. Then, the rabbi gave us the traditional Silver Chalice filled with wine to drink from. My mother took it upon herself to act as our sommelier. She poured a small bit of the wine into a cup which was attached to a chain hanging around her neck. After one taste, she sent it back for another vintage.

"What's-her-name's parents must have ordered that dreck," she whispered in my ear.

After we all got shickered, the rabbi read the marital vows. In the old days these vows were actually put into a written contractual form and signed by the bride and groom. Today, they need only be repeated before a group of relatives who can hardly wait for the chopped chicken liver to be passed around. When the rabbi came to the part, "If there are any objections why these two should not be wed, let it be said now, or forever hold your peace," my mother was about to raise her hand in protest. Fortunately, she was holding my hand at the time so I was able to restrain her.

Finally, the rabbi placed a wine glass wrapped in a handkerchief on the floor beside my foot. This "coup de gras" of Jewish wedding ceremonies dates back centuries. The smashing of the glass signifies the destruction of the Temple of Jerusalem. However, before I could even raise my foot, my mother had picked the glass up and was examining it closely.

"If my son wanted a cheap glass like this," she scolded the rabbi, "he would have registered at Woolworth."

My mother had even more fun planning our honeymoon. "I don't care where you go," she told me. "Just don't come home late for dinner."

When I explained we intended to go on a month-long honeymoon, she was a bit upset.

"But I couldn't possibly leave your father for that long a time," she protested.

SURVIVAL TIP #7

Always answer your mother's question with a question. Since a Jewish mother is an expert at asking questions, but not at answering them, she will get confused. Eventually, she will give up and leave you alone.

Eg: Mother: "Hilda's niece is such a nice girl. Why don't you take her out already?"

Son: "So, how is Hilda?"

Mother: "How should I know. I haven't seen Hilda in a month. But, I saw her niece at the supermarket. Is it such a crime to date a nice Jewish girl like her?"

Son: "You saw her niece? So, how was she feeling?"

Mother: "What am I, some kind of a doctor? Just forget it already!"

CHAPTER 18

WORRY, BE HAPPY!

T he secret to surviving a Jewish mother lies in understanding her thought processes. To truly appreciate this phenomenon of nature, I interviewed more than one hundred Jewish mothers, asking them a series of deep philosophical questions. The next few chapters will be devoted to exploring the results of that study.

One conclusion was irrefutable — all Jewish mothers think alike. When I started my interviews, the first thing they all said was, "Were you brought up in a barn? Get your feet off the furniture."

The Rorschach test was another example of their unified mind set. When I showed each of them a picture of two large, identical, irregularly shaped inkblots, half saw a picture of their son marrying a shiksa. The other half saw a picture of their daughter marrying a shaygets. This made two conclusions very clear: First, their biggest concern was their child marrying out of his or her faith and, second, they had hired terribly incompetent wedding photographers.

Their responses were so similar, it was as if they had all enrolled in the same school of child-rearing as soon as they became pregnant. If so, they would most assuredly graduate magna cum loud. And, my mother would be valedictorian of the class. I can hear her graduation speech now:

"My dear fellow graduates and canasta players. We have spent a wonderful nine months together, sharing belly laughs and belly pains. I will never forget the nights we sneaked out of the dormitory to eat chop suey a la mode. And, the days in class studying to be overprotective without making value judgments. But, now the time has come to acknowledge we will soon be bringing a defenseless child into this messugina world. A world which, on the one hand, is full of goyim who will want to marry them. And, on the other hand, goyim who will merely want to take advantage of them. Let us hope our children have the wisdom to make the right choice.

How we bring up our children will affect the future of Judaism. We can let them run helter skelter through life, or teach them that standing in a draft will surely result in a cold. The world is full of danger. One false move and they can be sued for malpractice. It is our maternal duty to worry about them all the time. Always remember, worry is contagious. It can be a great ally. The family that frets together, gets together. That is why it is so important to wait up until our child comes home at night. Now, my friends, as we leave these hallowed walls of ivy, let us join in singing the school song:

With heads held high, and bellies too, we sing the praise of Worry U."

The Jewish mother has turned worrying into an art

form. It has become the true measure of real love. She believes the more you worry about someone, the more you love them. And, she may have a point. Have you ever worried about someone you hated?

Worry U used Alfred E. Neumann as its prototype worrier. You remember the freckled faced youngster with the big ears who appeared in Mad Magazine. Alfred's favorite saying was, "What, me worry?" One look at Alfred's face and you knew he was a troubled Jew. Of course, if you looked like Alfred, you would worry too.

According to the teachings of Worry U, worrying is much like golf. Both can take up a whole day and accomplish nothing. However, unlike golf, worrying can be done indoors. In fact, it works better indoors, particularly on rainy days. Sunshine is not conducive to worrying, unless you want to worry about melanoma. As a bonus, worrying is absolutely free, and you don't even lose any golf balls. Jews are scratch worriers. The technique is passed on from generation to generation.

Worrying gives Jews a decided advantage in life. When an accident or misfortune occurs, the non-Jew is shocked and dismayed. This can lead them to act irrationally, perhaps causing even greater damage. On the other hand, a Jew laughs it off, saying "With my luck, I knew this would happen." In truth, he is relieved, because now that it's happened he can stop worrying about it.

The university's teachings, however, recommend multiple worries. Without a backup worry, the singular worrier is at risk. If the thing he is worrying about actually happens, he will face a serious void and may suffer withdrawal symptoms. Fortunately, scratch worriers can create new worries faster than you can say "Earthquake." An Earthquake, by the way, happens to be an excellent backup worry. The chance of one occurring in your neighborhood is remote. Consequently, you can worry about it indefinitely. And, if it happens, there is even a greater chance there will be a series of after-shocks. This is called a "regenerating worry," and all nationalities have one. For example, Haitians have hurricanes, Indonesians — typhoons, Japanese — tsunamis, Mexicans — diarrhea.

It is the Jewish mother's philosophy that life is too short to live in denial. Sooner or later adversity will strike. It is important to be mentally prepared. The secret to preparedness is "negative thinking."

The main ingredient of successful negative thinking is "tsuris." Tsuris is a Yiddish word which, translated, means trouble or woe. There is no singular for tsuris since it always comes in bulk. The word is most often used to describe a minor condition, rather than a major problem. In fact, it is well within the comfort zone of problems. If you hear a Jewish mother say, "Oy, have I got tsuris," chances are she hasn't found out she has leukemia, but more probably recently learned that her daughter is dating an Arab.

To fully appreciate her tsuris, we have to take a close look at her concern. Most non-Jews would assume the woman is concerned about mixed marriages and that her daughter will wind up divorced and miserable. In truth, the success or failure of an impending marriage is not paramount in her mind. What she is concerned about is having to introduce people to her grandson "Abdul." Certainly, many Jewish mothers would have no concern having a grandson named Abdul, though they might draw the line at Mohammed.

What is really important to recognize in the above illustration, is the Jewish mother in question created her own problem. She had the courage to step up to the plate of life, find a problem she believed in, and grab it with all the gusto she could muster. Therein lies the true power of negative thinking. On the surface, it may appear masochistic or paranoid. But, it is really intelligent and opportunistic. You see, life is full of continual problems. We can't avoid them any more than we can avoid death or Toyota commercials. Most of us expend all our energy running from problems that will eventually overtake us. While others suffer with problems heaped upon them by the juxtaposition of happenstance and fate, the Jewish mother glides through life with problems of her own choosing. Consequently, she has taken full control of her life.

Allow me to give you an everyday example which should make the value of this behavior abundantly clear. A person without money worries about how to make it. A person with money worries about how to keep it. The Jewish mother, on the other hand, worries about how to spend it. The fact is we are all destined to spend a good portion of our day worrying. So, we might as well spend it in Bloomingdale's.

CHAPTER 19

VIEW FROM A FRIDGE

There is an old wive's tale about the Jewish housewife who had two chickens. When one of the chickens got sick, she killed the well one to make chicken soup for the sick one. Of course this never happened. More probably, she killed both of them to make chopped chicken liver for her son's Bar Mitzvah. However, the tale illustrates the importance of food in the mind of the Jewish mother. Next to a good enema, food is her panacea of choice.

Today, there are more books written about health and fitness than any other subject. Barnes & Noble stocks more than 150 titles on "Diet" alone. Every thing from "Starving Your Way Through France On $300 a Day," to "How to Eat an Entire Suckling Pig and Lose Weight." All these books seem to be a big help when you read them, but 10 minutes later you are hungry for more information. They make excellent sense on paper, but it is impossible to digest all the information. If I could find a way to walk around all day with Dr. Dean Ornish in my pocket, I would be healthy and fit. Of course, I would also be 160 pounds heavier.

When I was growing up, there were no books like "The Eight Week Cholesterol Cure." My mother thought a cholesterol count was a royal title.

Everything she knew about food, she learned, not from books, but from her mother. And, the only book my grandmother ever read about food was entitled "Eat Something. Look At You, Leo," by Tolstoy's mother. My grandmother grew up in Russia, where everyone needed twenty pounds of extra weight to survive the brutal winters. A big tummy was evidence of a healthy, as well as, a wealthy person.

My mother still maintains that chopped chicken liver with schmaltz will make me strong and healthy. She suggests the surgeon general's food testing procedures are dubious at best. For example, the study that proves saccharin can cause cancer in laboratory rats.

"Are you aware that each rat was force-fed three times its own weight of saccharin daily," she told me. "If some giant rat in a white lab coat did that to me, cancer would be a great relief."

"And, just who is this surgeon general anyway?" she went on. "Is he a surgeon who specializes in operating on generals. Or is he a dyslexic general surgeon? I don't like someone I never met telling me what I should or shouldn't eat. I don't even know if the surgeon general keeps a kosher house."

As usual, my mother had a point. When she raised me, eating habits were a lot simpler. I ate everything on my plate because my mother told me 20 million Chinese were starving. I never really understood how finishing my dinner would help those poor folks. Wouldn't it have been better if I didn't finish the kreplach and sent them to the Chinese in a doggie bag. This was years before CNN, so there was no way of checking whether the Chinese were really starving. For all I knew, there might be Chinese mothers telling their children to finish their moo shu pork because 20 million American Jews were starving.

One time I asked my mother, "If there are 20 million Chinese starving, just name one of them." Without hesitating she shot back the name Marge Jongg. I later found out it was a game she played on Friday afternoons with her friends.

When I was growing up, food labels never contained the ingredients, but rather pictures of healthy, happy looking people. The determining factor of what to eat was not whether it might give you cancer, but whether it "agreed with you." No one likes to be contradicted by what one eats.

In those days, Jewish mothers did their own studies on the food their children should eat. A good example were the chicken soup studies of the '40s. Every Jewish mother knows chicken soup can cure every disease on the face of the earth except salmonella. But, how were they going to prove it to the masses. It would take the Food & Drug Administration a millennium to approve chicken soup as the world's panacea. Their scientists would have to deform a rat to the size of a Rottweiler just to get it to ingest three times it's body weight of the hot liquid.

Finally, the medicinal benefits of chicken soup were proven unequivocally by a simple experiment conducted by the Jewish FDA, the Fercockta Delicatessen Association. They reasoned the best way to prove the cure would be to make people terribly ill and then serve them chicken soup. So, they invented matzoh balls, a heinous concoction of unleavened bread and eggs, molded into a sphere the size of a tennis ball. The basic difference is that a tennis ball is easier to digest. In fact, a matzoh ball does not digest, it "nestles," and sits in the pit of your stomach until it dies of old age.

The proof was uncontestable. Add chicken soup to matzoh balls, creating matzoh ball soup, and not one subject got sick. No indigestion, no suffering and they all slept like babies. The world had no choice but to accept the proposition that, if chicken soup could mollify the effects of matzoh balls, then it could cure anything.

It was a momentous day for every Jewish mother when the results of the study were made public. Chicken soup was indeed Jewish penicillin. And, finally every Jewish mother in America could proudly say, "I told you so!"

CHAPTER 20

YOU DON'T HAVE TO BUY TICKETS FOR A GUILT TRIP

Guilt is a Jewish mothers weapon of choice. In fact, it is the mortar of Jewish civilization. It keeps us on the straight and narrow in the same manner as railroad tracks direct a train. Without Guilt, we might all wind up in Sioux City, Iowa.

As you can see, Guilt is always capitalized. This is not a typographical error. Rather, it represents the power of the word. A good example of its potency was when one of America's first astronauts, Hymie Schwartz, was about to fly Apollo One to the moon. Before leaving, his mother, Bertha, begged him not to go.

"It's dangerous up there." she extolled. "Who knows what's on the moon. What if it is inhabited by Anti-Semites."

In spite of her pleadings, Hymie lifted off. But, her words of foreboding rung in his ears. No sooner had the spacecraft left the earth's atmosphere than a tremendous urge to return home overtook Hymie's entire body. It was as if his mother was somehow pulling him back to earth. His reaction was recorded by sophisticated technical equipment at Space Headquarters in Houston. The NASA scientists quickly evaluated the behavior as a colossal guilt trip. The technical term for that behavior was thereafter termed "G Force."

In Jewish culture, Guilt has a quasi-pious nature. It has almost as much power and force as the other pious "G" word, though spelled backwards is not as amusing. In fact, God and Guilt have similar qualities. They are both omnipresent and omnipotent. That puts them right up there with Santa Claus, who, by the way, is rumored to have a Jewish brother-in-law.

Jewish mothers do not have a monopoly on Guilt. Catholics are also quite adept at using it beneficially. However, there are several differences between Jewish and Catholic Guilt. For one, Catholics have the opportunity to expunge themselves of Guilt by going to confessional, whereas Jews are stuck with Guilt for life. If I could feel better about having stolen that candy bar from Mr. Pimpkin's store when I was seven, I would be glad to throw five thousand Hail Marys, or whatever it is you do with them.

Second, Catholics impose Guilt only for major transgressions of God's words. Jews, on the other hand, invoke Guilt for mere misdemeanors — anything you do that your mother told you not to do. To this day, I feel guilty if I don't brush my teeth twice a day. Where is it written in the Bible "Thou shalt brush thy teeth." The great book does mention "a tooth for a tooth" but not in a hygienic sense. When I first encountered that phrase in Hebrew school, I thought God was teaching us not to mix apples and oranges. To trade a quid for a quid, not a quo. Then the Rabbi explained it was The Lord's way of telling us it was okay to be vindictive so long as you do not get too overzealous about it. If someone kicks you in the shin, you can kick him back, but don't aim higher.

Later, I learned that God had a strange concept of "equal force." When, against God's dictate, Lot's wife looked back at Sodom and Gomorrah, God decided to teach her a lesson so he changed her into a pillar of salt. She was so upset she immediately disavowed her faith and started the Shaker religion.

Some of you less pious folks may look at what God did to Lot's wife as a cheap shot. But, God was only using Lot's wife to set an example. Heed my words or you too may become a condiment. If a whole town defies God he has been known to get so angry that he will destroy it by setting off a volcano. And that's just the appetizer. Eternal Hell is the main course.

A Jewish mother is much subtler in getting her way. She doesn't have to use famine or plague to make a point. In fact, she doesn't do anything at all. You do it to yourself. After a few chosen words such as "After all I've done for you," Vesuvius falls smack on your head. This phenomenon is best explained by Dr. Isadore Pfuffnick in his famous treatise, "You Don't Buy Tickets for a Guilt Trip." He conducted two simultaneous studies which established the same result.

In the Spring of 1969, Dr. Pfuffnick studied the

behavioral patterns of 40 children ages 8 thru 11 in Brooklyn. Half of the youngsters were from middle-class Jewish homes. The other half were children of Italian immigrants. None of the youths was aware the study was being conducted. Each day a valuable object, such as a camera or a watch, was conspicuously left where each child could steal it. When the studies were completed, it was interesting to learn that both the Jewish and Italian children took almost an equal amount of objects. This occurred in spite of the Jewish mothers reminding their children daily that it was wrong to steal.

However, three months later, the Italian children were joyfully playing with their new-found valuables. The Jewish children, on the other hand, were all noticeably unhappy and depressed. This was in spite of the fact they had opened up a very successful pawn shop on Flatbush Avenue.

Dr. Pfuffnick was impacted by the fact the Jewish children felt remorse even though they had never been chastised directly by their mothers for the thefts. It was sufficient for the child to know the mother would disapprove of his behavior if she was aware of it. After some psychoanalysis, Dr. Pfuffnick found out the Jewish children were suffering from depression. It was their way of paying penance for not having listened to their mother.

Dr. Pfuffnick concluded that Guilt was the confessional of the Jewish religion. The children entered the penalty box in their minds, where they confessed their crimes and received absolution.

Dr. Pfuffnick's second study was equally enlightening. He divided 20 orphaned boys into two groups. One group was placed in families with a Jewish mother. The other group was given a placebo. They were placed in homes with non-Jewish mothers who pretended to be Jewish. Although the study is ongoing, one result already is clear. The children in Jewish households received much more expensive gifts for their Bar Mitzvah than their counterparts. Perhaps this was due to the fact that many of the boys from non-Jewish homes had their Bar Mitzvah performed by the janitor during study hall.

Dr. Pfuffnick concluded from the combined studies that the behavior of Jewish mothers cannot be artificially duplicated. It is a genetic phenomenon passed from mother to daughter.

The famed genealogist, Calvin Kline, takes exception to Dr. Pfuffnick's conclusion, and insists it is too simplistic.

"It is too easy to blame our genes for all of our actions," Kline suggests.

Kline believes the problem is that science cannot yet determine which genes we will inherit. He says that, unfortunately, studies confirm our negative genes are more resilient than our positive ones. To confuse matters even more, some genes skip a generation or two before reappearing. Muscular dystrophy, for example, appears every third generation, making it difficult to track. Luckily, congenital heart disease passes directly from parent to child so we have something to look forward to. Of course, there are a few positive genes, such as longevity, which pass directly to one's offspring. However, they are quite worthless if you die young.

The Guilt gene, on the other hand, doesn't skip generations. In fact, it doesn't skip a day. It is God's way of saying, "Listen to your mother."

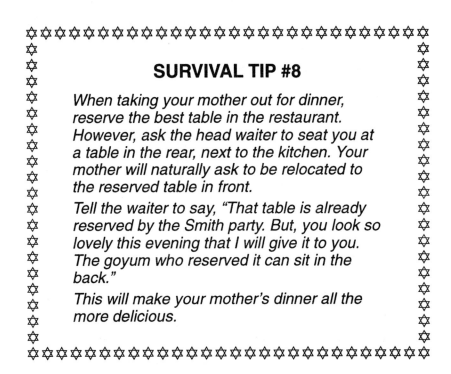

SURVIVAL TIP #8

When taking your mother out for dinner, reserve the best table in the restaurant. However, ask the head waiter to seat you at a table in the rear, next to the kitchen. Your mother will naturally ask to be relocated to the reserved table in front.

Tell the waiter to say, "That table is already reserved by the Smith party. But, you look so lovely this evening that I will give it to you. The goyum who reserved it can sit in the back."

This will make your mother's dinner all the more delicious.

CHAPTER 21

GREAT JEWISH MOTHERS THROUGHOUT HISTORY

C ontrary to the dictates of Dr. Pfuffnick and other experts, it is apparent that one doesn't have to be Jewish to have a Jewish mother. Any overprotective matriarch can fill the bill. All it takes is a mother who believes that, without her constant vigil, her son or daughter will surely get into trouble. Italian mothers, for example, are great Jewish mothers. However, they cook much better lasagna.

History is replete with great Jewish mothers who have been subtly responsible for their children's successes. After exhaustive research, I have put together a number of quotes from Jewish mothers throughout history, which I list below in no particular order.

"Stop playing with matches, you're liable to set something on fire."
Nero's mother.

"What's with those symbols. Can't you write like a normal person."
Einstein's mother.

"Get down from that ladder. You could get a nose bleed."
                    Sir Edmond Hillary's mother.

"Don't spend all your time indoors. Why don't you go outside and fly a kite or something."
                    Ben Franklin's mother

"Stop throwing all that paint around. You'll soil the carpet."
                    Jackson Pollack's mother

"I don't care how much you love him. He's a WASP."
                    Pocahontas's mother

"At least pick up the phone and call once in a while."
                    Alexander Graham Bell's mother

"I'm going to sit right here until you come home."
                    Whistler's mother

"How can you expect to be a success only working one day a year."
                    Santa Claus's mother

"I hardly recognize you anymore."

Michael Jackson's mother

"Go take a long nap. You look exhausted."

Rip Van Winkle's mother

"And what bright idea have you come up with now."

Thomas Edison's mother

"You drive me crazy."

Mario Andretti's mother

"Get a nose job, already."

Barbara Streisand's mother

"If your father finds you dressed like that, he'll have a conniption."

Peter Pan's mother

"Funny, you don't look Jewish."

Sammy Davis Jr.'s mother

"Eat something, look at you."

Ghandi's mother

But, perhaps the best historical example of a Jewish mother's influence on her offspring is Napoleon's mother. In his memoirs entitled "Short Subjects," the General relates the time his mother took him shopping at a ritzy Champs Elysee store. In the window, she saw a beautifully tailored navy blue vest for 5000 francs her son would look dashing in.

"5000 francs!" she exclaims to the proprietor, Lou Goldberg. "Mrs. Wellington bought her son one just like it from you for 3000 francs."

"That's true," Lou responds, "but the Duke wears an X-tra large and it was on sale."

"When do you put the smalls on sale?"

"I'm afraid we never put the smalls or mediums on sale, Madam."

"Suppose we buy an X-tra large and have it taken in?"

"Sorry, Madam, but the Duke bought our last X-tra large. However, you may be in luck. We do have an irregular small in the back which the tailor forgot to put pockets in. I can let you have it for 3000 francs."

"Make it 2000 and we'll take it off your hands." Napoleon's mother counters. "If my son's hands get cold, he can always put them inside the vest."

Mrs. Bonaparte exhibited what is commonly referred to in Jewish culture as the "markdown instinct." Henny Youngman expressed it best when his wife came home one day with an escalator. "She'll buy anything marked DOWN," he remarked. For a Jewish mother, this "Call of the Bargain" is as compelling as Jack London's' Call of the Wild, Capt. Ahab's Call of the Sea, or Johnny's Call for Philip Morris.

In a recent survey of 100 Jewish women, more than three-fourths did not know the meaning of the word "retail," whereas only one didn't know what a "White Flower Day" was, and she was color-blind. Jewish mothers believe people who buy retail are throwing money away. Of course, those people also wear clothes that fit.

The true thrill of the bargain, however, is not in saving money, but rather in buying something cheaper than someone else. It is a shopper's one-upmanship. Mrs. Bonaparte was not the first to exhibit this trait and she certainly was not the last. If Noah's mother hadn't found a great "going out of business sale" at Bethlehem Lumber & Dry Goods, her son could not have built the Ark. Gabriel's mother bought his horn for a song at the flea market. And history repeats itself every day at Loehmann's.

CHAPTER 22

MY SON WHAT'S HIS NAME

A Jewish mother's Golden Years are a time to reap the rewards of the seeds she has sown. This is commonly referred to in the Jewish vernacular as "After all I've done for you."

Most Jewish children find this phrase to be a guilt trip, but nothing could be further from the truth. Her intention is not to make her children feel guilty, but rather to receive fair and equitable compensation for her efforts to date. And she isn't even asking for anything important. That is why the phrase always continues with "...the least you can do is..."

Let's be fair here. If there was a Jewish Mothers Union, don't you think they would get retirement benefits far in excess of what they presently have. You bet they would. In fact, if all the Jewish mothers in America decided to go out on strike, the medical profession would stand still and the law courts would have to close. The trucking industry, on the other hand, wouldn't be affected in the least. However, a strong Jewish Mothers Union would make the AFL-CIO seem like a daisy chain.

I was so appreciative of the work my mother had done for me that, when I turned 25, I presented her with a gold pocket watch. Inscribed inside were the words, "For 25 years of meritorious service. Yes, I brushed my teeth this morning." She was so pleased that she dropped the age discrimination suit she had filed against me.

This is not to say that, when a Jewish mother's children reach the age of maturity, her work is finished. Quite the contrary, although her job description does change to "Supervisor." No longer does she work hands-on in the assembly line of life. Now she can sit back and judge how badly your spouse is treating you. The first month after Samantha and I got married, my mother sent her three pink slips.

A Jewish mother reaches the pinnacle of her career when she becomes a grandmother. Then, her years of experience really come into play. As a supervisor, her job is to test her own child's ability to be a quality parent. This she does by totally spoiling her grandchild and observing how her child handles the situation.

In this regard, an interesting research study was conducted by Yeshiva University in the winter of 1962. Forty Jewish children, between the age of 3 and 6, were divided into two groups. Group Alpha was given expensive gifts by their grandmothers on each day for the eight days of Hanukkah. Group Bravo was given a placebo, which consisted of attractively gift wrapped boxes with nothing inside. On the ninth day, when no gifts were forthcoming, the Group Alpha children cried uncontrollably. The children in Group Bravo, on the other hand, appeared relaxed, even relieved.

Twenty years later the study evaluated the various children who were now young adults. Those who had been in Group Alpha all had Type A personalities. Those in Group Bravo were normal and well adjusted, even though they had converted en masse to Catholicism as soon as the initial study was completed.

As a grandparent, the Jewish mother is at the top of her game. By constantly imparting information and ideas in the fertile mind of her grandchildren, she can maintain a presence in the family for generations to come. She can leave footprints in the family's sandbox.

However, one day we look at our mother and see that the Golden Years have turned into the Olden Years. We notice she really can't remember our spouse's name. Suddenly, she refers to everyone as "What's-her-name." She no longer tells us to wear a sweater or we'll catch cold. Or to chew our food well so we don't choke like poor Uncle Ruby.

For our entire adult life we have told our mother, "Cut it out. Stop treating me like a baby, mom." At last, she has done just that. And, you know the funny part. We miss it terribly.

A JEWISH MOTHER'S DICTIONARY OF TERMS

Contrary to what many may believe, the Jewish lexicon is not a small fellow with large, pointed ears, who runs around in green tights yelling "Top of the mornin' to ya, rabbi." Rather, it is the Yiddish language. Hebrew is also the language of the Jewish people, but I haven't spoken a word of it since I was 13. Yiddish, on the other hand, I speak almost every day. That is mostly because my boss is such a schmuck. The Yiddish lexicon has become so imbedded in American speech that most people say some Yiddish words regularly. That is because most people have a boss who is a schmuck.

Yiddish, which is a concoction of Hebrew, German, Slavic and a number of other European languages, is pronounced best by someone with a bad head cold. Listed below are a Jewish mother's English definitions of Yiddish words used in this book. Spelling of words may vary depending on whether she is using a milchedika or a flayshedika spell checker.

Bar Mitzvah: The ceremony, held in a temple, in which a 13 year old boy gives a speech in a language he doesn't understand to a bunch of relatives he's never seen before.

Blintzes: Jewish cannelloni.

Boychick: A baby rooster.

Briss: The cutting-edge ceremony performed on an eight day old Jewish male.

Bubkes: What is left of a Jewish baby's private part after the briss.

Cantor: A frustrated Jewish opera singer.

Cheder: A good place for a young Jewish child to spend a Sunday if he doesn't live in a city with an NFL team.

Chutzpa: Telling your boss that he's a schmuck.

Delicatessen: A restaurant in which all the waiters are elderly and hard of hearing.

Enema: The number one Jewish panacea.

Fercockta: Someone rowing a boat upstream with one oar.

Gefilte fish: A fish stuffed to the gills.

Gevalt: The expletive for "Oy."

Goy: Anyone who thinks a yarmulkah is a string instrument.

Goyum: A bevy of goys.

Goyisha Kup: Someone who buys their clothes retail.

Guilt: A basic Jewish emotion which has been popularized by modern psychiatry.

Hanukkah: Or Hanuka, or Hanukah, or Chanukah, or Channukah. The only religious holiday in the world today that nobody can agree on how to spell.

Haymish: A white home-boy.

Knish: The Jewish answer to a Napoleon.

Kreplach: Jewish pot stickers.

Latkas: Potato pancakes for people with a death wish.

Loehmanns: Ross for Jews

Lox: Something you put on a bagel to keep it from being stolen.

Matzoh: A loaf of bread suffering from impotence.

Matzoh Balls: A cure for Tagamet.

Menorah: A silver candle holder with between seven and nine stems, depending on whether you buy it at Hammacker Schlemmer or the Price Club.

Meshuggina: A crazy person from Michigan

Mezuzah: A sign on a door indicating the occupants do not play polo.

Mishpocheh: People who appear magically when a will is being read.

Mohel: Someone who always gets the point.

Naches: A Jewish-Mexican appetizer.

Oy: The harbinger of a problem.

Putz: A schmuck with an attitude.

Rebbe: A Southern rabbi.

Schmaltz: Money in the bank for companies selling cholesterol lowering drugs.

Schmuck: Your boss.

Seder: An anorexic's worst nightmare.

Shalom: Can mean hello or goodbye, depending on which way you are walking.

Shegetz: Someone you don't want your daughter to marry.

Shicksa: Someone you don't want your son to marry.

Shvartza: Someone you don't want your son or daughter to marry.

Shlep: To drag something heavy over a long distance when you could have taken a taxi.

Shmageggie: A Jewish dork.

Tefillin: A non-stick morning prayer shawl.

Tsuris: A problem that grows significantly in the telling.

Vay iz mier: Literally, "woe is me." Put "oy" in front, and you have tsuris.

Yeshiva: A Jewish seminary or educational facility with a lousy football team.

Yiddishe kup: Anyone who buys this book.

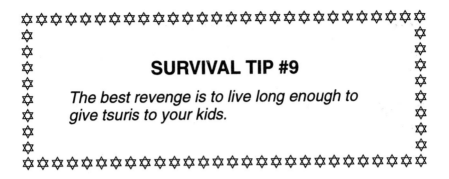

SURVIVAL TIP #9

The best revenge is to live long enough to give tsuris to your kids.

ABOUT THE AUTHOR

At a very early age, Steven Arnold was born in New York City. Moments before his briss, he decided to convert to Agnosticism. His mother, however, did not give her approval. Since that time he has been on the cutting edge, but has always come up a little bit short. Writing How to Survive a Jewish Mother is his way of evening the score for all those who have experienced a similar fate. Furthermore, he is convinced this book will tickle everybody's funny bone. Even those who think that the Borscht Belt is something to hold your pants up.

TITLES BY CCC PUBLICATIONS

Retail $4.99
"?" book
POSITIVELY PREGNANT
SIGNS YOUR SEX LIFE IS DEAD
WHY MEN DON'T HAVE A CLUE
CAN SEX IMPROVE YOUR GOLF?
THE COMPLETE BOOGER BOOK
THINGS YOU CAN DO WITH A USELESS MAN
FLYING FUNNIES
MARITAL BLISS & OXYMORONS
THE VERY VERY SEXY ADULT DOT-TO-DOT BOOK
THE DEFINITIVE FART BOOK
THE COMPLETE WIMP'S GUIDE TO SEX
THE CAT OWNER'S SHAPE UP MANUAL
PMS CRAZED: TOUCH ME AND I'LL KILL YOU!
RETIRED: LET THE GAMES BEGIN
MALE BASHING: WOMEN'S FAVORITE PASTIME
THE OFFICE FROM HELL
FOOD & SEX
FITNESS FANATICS
YOUNGER MEN ARE BETTER THAN RETIN-A
BUT OSSIFER, IT'S NOT MY FAULT

Retail $4.95
1001 WAYS TO PROCRASTINATE
THE WORLD'S GREATEST PUT-DOWN LINES
HORMONES FROM HELL II
SHARING THE ROAD WITH IDIOTS

THE GREATEST ANSWERING MACHINE MESSAGES
OF ALL TIME
WHAT DO WE DO NOW?? (A Guide For New Parents)
HOW TO TALK YOU WAY OUT OF A TRAFFIC TICKET
THE BOTTOM HALF (How To Spot Incompetent
Professionals)
LIFE'S MOST EMBARRASSING MOMENTS
HOW TO ENTERTAIN PEOPLE YOU HATE
YOUR GUIDE TO CORPORATE SURVIVAL
THE SUPERIOR PERSON'S GUIDE TO EVERYDAY
IRRITATIONS
GIFTING RIGHT
YOU KNOW YOU'RE AN OLD FART WHEN...

Retail $5.95
40 AND HOLDING YOUR OWN
50 AND HOLDING YOUR OWN
LITTLE INSTRUCTION BOOK OF THE RICH & FAMOUS
GETTING EVEN WITH THE ANSWERING MACHINE
ARE YOU A SPORTS NUT?
MEN ARE PIGS / WOMEN ARE BITCHES
50 WAYS TO HUSTLE YOUR FRIENDS ($5.99)
HORMONES FROM HELL
HUSBANDS FROM HELL
KILLER BRAS & Other Hazards Of The 50's
IT'S BETTER TO BE OVER THE HILL THAN UNDER IT
HOW TO REALLY PARTY!!!
WORK SUCKS!
THE PEOPLE WATCHER'S FIELD GUIDE
THE UNOFFICIAL WOMEN'S DIVORCE GUIDE
THE ABSOLUTE LAST CHANCE DIET BOOK
FOR MEN ONLY (How To Survive Marriage)

THE UGLY TRUTH ABOUT MEN
NEVER A DULL CARD

RED HOT MONOGAMY
   (In Just 60 Seconds A Day) ($6.95)
HOW TO SURVIVE A JEWISH MOTHER ($6.95)
WHY MEN DON'T HAVE A CLUE ($7.99)
LADIES, START YOUR ENGINES! ($7.99)

Retail $3.95
NO HANG-UPS
NO HANG-UPS II
NO HANG-UPS III
HOW TO SUCCEED IN SINGLES BARS
HOW TO GET EVEN WITH YOUR EXES
TOTALLY OUTRAGEOUS BUMPER-SNICKERS ($2.95)

NO HANG-UPS – CASSETTES Retail $4.98
Vol. I: GENERAL MESSAGES (Female)
Vol. I: GENERAL MESSAGES (Male)
Vol. II: BUSINESS MESSAGES (Female)
Vol. II: BUSINESS MESSAGES (Male)
Vol. III: 'R' RATED MESSAGES (Female)
Vol. III: 'R' RATED MESSAGES (Male)
Vol. IV: SOUND EFFECTS ONLY
Vol. V: CELEBRI-TEASE